Caleb the

A mother's story of hope

Laura Griswold

Caleb the Conqueror

Author: Laura Griswold
Foreword: Andy Griswold
Editor: Lori Kenney, Marla McKenna
Proofreader: Lyda Rose Haerle, Laura Griswold
Cover Painting: Caleb Griswold
Cover Design: Laura Griswold
Interior & Cover Layout: Griffin Mill

All images are courtesy of Laura Griswold unless otherwise noted. Additional photographs by Mike Roemer, ROEMERPHOTO (Guideposts); Jeff Frings, Fox (Caleb's World); David Fischer, Realife Photography; Colleen Jurkiewicz, *News Graphic*; Edwin Gonzalez (@Soy_edwin25); Jennifer Ziegler, Hope Lake Creative; Adrian Spinks, Arts Mill; and John Urban, Big Dreamers United (bigdreamersunited.org).

Note—Some of the names in this book have been changed to protect privacy.

ISBN: 978-1-957351-29-2

PUBLISHED BY NICO 11 PUBLISHING & DESIGN
MUKWONAGO, WISCONSIN
www.nico11publishing.com

Quantity order requests can be emailed to:
mike@nico11publishing.com

Printed in The United States of America

Our family was utterly devastated by Caleb's diagnosis. Caleb's unfolding story is an inspirational testimony about how God uses Caleb's childlike faith, determination, and cheerful outlook to impact lives beyond our hopes and dreams. Some families are just beginning their journey. Our prayer is that they will find hope in seeing how God fortified us and paved the way for Caleb to become independent and develop his gifts to be used for His glory. From a mother's perspective, my heart's prayer is that others may gain insight, encouragement, and practical strategies to be lifelong advocates.

Dedication

*Remember your leaders, who spoke the word of God to you.
Consider the outcome of their way of life and imitate their faith.*

Hebrews 13:7

I dedicate Caleb the Conqueror to my mother, Pat Just, who faithfully and lovingly poured into me as a little girl, guided me as a young adult, and walked with me through weary days of motherhood. Her godly example as a prayer warrior equipped me to draw my strength from the Lord and give Him praise amidst the joys and challenges of life, knowing all of it will be used for His glory.

Foreword

A Father's Heart

I will instruct you and teach you in the way you should go;
I will counsel you with My loving eye on you.
Psalm 32:8

This book is a beautiful read about life with a beautiful soul. As Caleb's dad, I have always wanted to "fix" his brain condition to make everything "better" for everyone, but I came to the realization that he is perfect in his own way. God made him the way he is for a purpose. Before Laura and 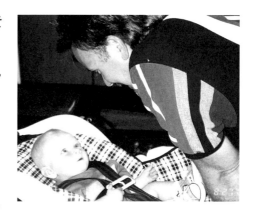 I got married and had kids, she knew she was going to have or be involved with a special needs child.

I'm not sure why, but the thought of it was my worst nightmare. On the contrary, my life with Caleb has been a very special one, and I can't imagine my life without him.

–Andy

Table of Contents

Caleb the Conqueror

In all these things we are more than conquerors through Him who loved us.

Romans 8:37

Caleb is a Conqueror. Miraculously, he defeats many odds and lives his life unhindered, without abandon, and to the fullest. From the beginning, my prayer-warrior mom prayed over and spoke truth into him, calling him Caleb the Conqueror. By the grace of God, Caleb conquered walking. He conquered talking. He conquered fine motor skills and many other aspects of his diagnosis. Whether a smile, a prayer, a bear hug, a heartfelt card, or a helping hand, the Holy Spirit uses Caleb in powerful ways to touch people's hearts and souls.

The honors and accolades Caleb has received are impressive: Extraordinary Citizen of the Year, Ozaukee Impact Award - Volunteer of the Year, Mayor of Muttland Meadows, Artist-in-Residence, self-employed artist for Paintings and Paws by Caleb. But to know his humble servant's heart is even more endearing.

At 23 years old, Caleb has a fulfilling life, but he started with enormous challenges even before he came into this world. Nothing could have prepared us for the journey ahead, but our faith and trust in the Lord and leaning on His wisdom for guidance and direction continue to carry us through.

Our journey embraces many blessings, heartaches, questions, fears, tears, despair, devastation, and jubilation. Our journey meanders through many stages of life, but the common thread woven throughout is this—God is faithful and continues to direct our path.

Preparation

Trust in the Lord with all your heart
and lean not on your own understanding;
in all your ways acknowledge Him and He will direct your path.

Proverbs 3:5-6

Even though I didn't know it, God prepared my heart for motherhood when I was a young girl. My fifth grade teacher, Mrs. Just, was my distant cousin who profoundly impacted my life. She did not put restraints on my creativity. She allowed me to turn everything into an art project...spelling lists, stories, and history projects. In fifth grade, I knew I wanted to be a teacher *just* like her.

When I was 13 years old, my mom and I watched *Son-Rise: A Miracle of Love*, a 1979 TV movie. It was about a severely unresponsive autistic boy. The boy demonstrated little progress, but as his mom entered his world and tirelessly poured all she had into him, he responded! The pure joy and reward she received when he communicated his desire for orange juice made such an impact on me as a little girl. God used this movie to stir a passion for helping people with special needs have a breakthrough. I remember telling my mom was what I wanted to do. It is one of those moments etched in my heart and soul.

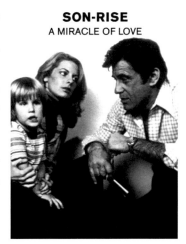

SON-RISE
A MIRACLE OF LOVE

BROWN HOUSE WITH A WINDMILL

When I was in high school, my sister, Lynda, asked me to pick her up from her friend's house. Since we had recently moved to Germantown, Wisconsin, I was unfamiliar with the area, but her vague directions seemed easy enough, so off I went. After I exited the highway, it didn't take long before I realized I was completely lost. As I ventured up and down the steep hills, I began to panic because I was almost out of gas in the middle of nowhere and had no money! In desperation, I stopped at a farm to ask for help, but two large, unruly dogs bounded toward me, scaring me back into my car. I turned around and headed back to the highway, praying I would not run out of gas. Searching for anyone to help me, I turned onto the frontage road and slowly drove into a trailer court. I was so relieved when a friendly man playing catch with his son asked if I needed help. Flustered, I told him I was completely lost, I didn't have an address, and all I knew was that I was looking for a brown house with a windmill.

He responded, "I have a brown house with a windmill. Who are you looking for?"

"My sister, Lynda." "Oh, Lynda. Yes, she's right in the house. I will go get her."

What?? Are you kidding me? I was at the exact house that I needed to be! I was in complete shock! Moments ago, I was frantic, wondering how I would ever find my sister, and now relief washed over me. The minor detail of being a trailer home was missing in the directions! The kind father gave us gas money and sent us on our way!

Throughout my life, I look back on that experience as an example of the Lord directing my path. As I grow in my relationship and trust Him, He leads me. Even though I may feel lost, empty, and attacked, He faithfully guides me through it.

After high school, I attended Trinity Bible College in Ellendale, North Dakota. Those were foundational years of deepening my faith and trust in the Lord. We were surrounded by godly friends and immersed in prayer while waiting for God's prompting to direct our lives. I knew I wanted to be a teacher, but I also felt God leading me toward special education. I remember sitting in my dorm room at TBC and telling my roommate I felt I would have a special needs child. It wasn't a devastating thought to me, though. God, in His graciousness, prepared me for Caleb long before he was born. After two years at TBC, I left my cherished friends and comfort zone and transferred to

the University of Wisconsin-LaCrosse to receive an elementary major and special education and psychology minors.

While I was at UW-LaCrosse, God used a dear family to prepare me to work with special needs children. Shirley and Roger dedicated their lives to raising their children, including adopted children with special needs. Stacy had cerebral palsy, the other Stacey (both had the same name) was cognitively disabled, and Matt has spina bifida.

Two weekends a month, I worked at their house as a respite care provider for Stacy, Stacey, and Matt so Shirley and Roger could have some time to themselves. We spent our days singing worship songs while I played my guitar. We baked cookies and bonded around the kitchen table. Shirley had a powerful impact on me as I watched her engage with her adopted daughters. The girls loved Jesus because they saw Shirley's love for Jesus. Since I was there from the moment the girls awoke, I experienced firsthand what was required to get them out of a wet bed, bathed, dressed, and entertained for a long time. It was not always glamorous, but it filled my soul. It was a natural fit for me. Caring for this family was preparation woven into the tapestry of God's design.

Caleb often carries himself with the tightness of cerebral palsy, and much of his care is not glamorous, but he has the same sweet spirit as Stacy. They are not bogged down or stressed about life. They live in the moment, unhindered, and love Jesus.

After graduation, I was a case manager at Developmental Achievement Center for special needs adults; it was my first job. This experience was valuable and memorable. Our job was to ride the bus, pick up the special needs adults at the group home, and take them to the center. Once at the center, we worked with individuals at their jobs. Here I learned to meet people where they were and celebrate their gifts.

Our favorite time of the day was when we took the morning bus from the group home to the center. The bus driver engaged everyone by name.

"Blake, wind up the bus," as Blake made a big rotation with his arm.

Suzie squealed with delight as he yelled, "Suzie, sound the backup alarm!"

Everyone had something to contribute. We had fun and experienced community on what could have been a very monotonous ride. I often look back at that time, realizing that experience impacted my life. Living with Caleb is a joy when I live in the moment and turn life into an adventure or a fun game.

Falling in Love

~wedding verse~
By wisdom, a house is built, and through understanding it is established; through knowledge its rooms are filled with rare and beautiful treasures.
Proverbs 24:3

My husband Andy and I met at church. I was in the choir, and Andy was the "sound guy." We lived on Milwaukee's East Side, only a few blocks from each other. Initially, I thought he was married, so when I saw Andy walking down the sidewalk with a gallon of milk, I thought, *Darn, I missed out on this nice guy getting a gallon of milk for his wife.* To my surprise and delight, he was single and available.

I fell in love with Andy on our first date at Lisa's Pizza. There was an ease and comfort about him, and our backgrounds were similar. Since we grew up near each other and went to neighboring youth groups, we were both at the same concerts and Christian skate nights as teenagers. We were very compatible; opposites attract! Andy's demeanor is calm and steady, whereas I am exuberant and spontaneous, and my zeal for life can sometimes get carried away. In my heart of hearts, I knew on our first date that I would marry him. During our romantic Valentine's Day dinner a few months later, Andy commented "Maybe next year at this time…" I don't know if or how he finished his sentence, but he was implying that we might get married in a year. My mind immediately raced to, *If he's thinking Valentine's Day, we might as well move it up to Christmas because I always wanted a Christmas*

wedding. The venues fill up fast; I better get on that!

While he was on a hunting trip, I called the church and the restaurant and booked a "Just Griswold" wedding! Since December had already filled up for both venues, I booked a November wedding. Imagine Andy's surprise when he returned from his hunting trip, and I told him I had just booked our wedding for the following November, right during hunting season! He had not even proposed yet, but his response was that I would be his "dear" that year. My sister-in-law later reminded me that our anniversary would be during hunting season every year, so I called back both the restaurant and the church; thankfully, they both had cancellations for a December wedding. On December 2, 1995, we had an elegant Christmas wedding filled with love, promise, and grateful hearts!

The Ultrasound

You created my inmost being; You knit me together in my mother's womb.
I praise you because I am fearfully and wonderfully made;
your works are wonderful, I know that full well.
My frame was not hidden from You when I was made in the secret
place, when I was woven together in the depths of the earth. Your eyes
saw my unformed body; all the days ordained for me were written
in Your book before one of them came to be.
Psalm 139:13-16

Andy and I were building our sweet life together. We were over the moon when I found out I was pregnant four years later. We knew it was a miracle I was able to get pregnant!

"Young lady, do you know how fortunate you are!" exclaimed the doctor, "Countless ladies come into my office with endometriosis and never get pregnant."

I never told Andy I always felt I would have a child with special needs. He later revealed that it was always his greatest fear…

I loved every part of being pregnant. I wore an oversized jumper the day we found out. Our friends were having babies, but finally, we would welcome our own child! I craved tuna, watermelon, salad with rotisserie chicken, cheese, peas, and French dressing. Andy finished the bedroom suite in our bungalow to make way for our new arrival. The nursery was decorated with an adorable teddy bear crib blanket and blue checkerboard sheets. All of my doctor appointments were normal. Andy came to the ultrasounds with me as we were both so excited. Everything was perfect.

Everything that is until two weeks before I was supposed to deliver our precious baby. I went to my doctor's appointment, and since everything was going smoothly, Andy didn't come to the appointment. After the doctor examined me, he believed the baby was breech. He wanted an ultrasound immediately. I wasn't too concerned because I didn't care if the baby was coming upside down; all I cared about was that the baby was coming. The technician and I chatted about baby names as the cool gel trickled on my belly. She clicked and took measurements in the dark room as I babbled about the baby's arrival. After the gel was wiped off, I quickly dressed and waited to hear if our baby was coming breech.

The door opened, and the nurse matter-of-factly told me, "The doctor would like to see you in his office." My heart skipped a beat, "Okay." I had never been in his office before, but, okay…I felt vulnerable and nervous, sensing that he would drop a bomb. In his calm demeanor, and as gently as he could, the doctor delivered the devastating news from his heart to mine, "The baby has cerebral swelling."

"What does that mean?" I questioned.

"Fluid on the brain…" he replied.

"WHAT DOES THAT MEAN?" I repeated with sheer panic.

He responded with fatherly love and urgency as he picked up his phone, "I don't know, but you're going to see a specialist immediately." The moment's intensity was so palpable that it took my breath away.

I immediately called Andy and cried my heart out. I couldn't even utter a word; I just sobbed uncontrollably. He thought we had lost the baby because I couldn't talk, so he was relieved to hear the baby was still alive. Angels surrounded me on the drive home to get Andy because I don't even remember how I got there.

Andy, always the calm one amid a storm, was my rock. Our hearts were devastated and scared as we immediately rushed to a geneticist. As the genetics specialist spoke, with his thick German accent and compassion in his voice, we clung to every word. He rattled off the possibilities of spina bifida, cerebral palsy, and other devastating diagnoses. With wisdom and empathy, he drew a box and told us not to fill in the box until we knew more after our baby was born. My unspoken fear was that our baby's head would be monstrously deformed, so the doctor's parting words, "Tiger has a cute face," brought great comfort. He told us to go home and relax for two weeks until our baby was born.

I had heard that the salad dressing at the Olive Garden put mothers into labor, so in shock, we headed to the Olive Garden to no avail. As devastating as the news was, the Lord wrapped His arms around us with an indescribable peace during those two weeks as believers stormed the gates of heaven on behalf of our baby.

Chapter Resource:

Son-Rise Program

https://autismtreatmentcenter.org/what-is-the-son-rise-program

Caleb's Birth

I praise You because I am fearfully and wonderfully made;
Your works are wonderful. I know that full well.

Psalm 139:14

On Monday, April 10, 2000, Caleb Andrew was born. He looked perfectly healthy; Tiger did have a cute face! The delivery went well. The specialists were all on hand, but thankfully, a shunt was not necessary. We all held hands in the room, including the doctor and nurses. My mom prayed, "Lord God, ten lepers were healed, but only one returned to give thanks. All ten of us in this room want to give thanks for this little gift from You!"

Caleb was a nine-pound baby boy placed in the ICU with many tiny premature babies. He did not look like he belonged, but sadly, we knew he did.

Caleb's baby picture is a testimony of God's healing miracle. His fingers were visibly tight and cramped at birth; they needed to be stretched to eventually relax. Twenty years later, we marvel at Caleb's ease of creating colorful strokes of beauty with a fine detail paintbrush.

A Different Spirit

The name Caleb means wholehearted, bold, and brave. We named our Caleb after Caleb in the Bible, but we had no idea how fitting and encouraging his name would become.

In Numbers 13, the Israelites were just freed from 400 years of slavery in Egypt. Moses led them to the border of Canaan, the Promised Land. The Lord told Moses to send 12 spies into Canaan to explore it. After 40 days of scouting the land, they returned home and gave a report. The 12 spies agreed on the description of the rich and fertile land flowing with milk and honey. It took two men to carry a single cluster of grapes on the pole! But they said the people who live there are powerful giants. We seem like grasshoppers to them. Ten of the spies gave a negative report.

However, only two, Caleb and Joshua, came back with a positive report. Caleb said, *We should go up and take possession of the land, for we can certainly do it.* – Numbers 13:30. They all saw the same things, but it was how they *interpreted* them.

The Lord told them to go in and conquer the land, but ten were looking at the circumstances. Because of their negative report, the Israelites tore their clothes in despair and discouragement. They wanted to go back to Egypt, even though the Lord had demonstrated His faithfulness by miraculously delivering them from slavery by parting the Red Sea. He directed them by day with a pillar of cloud and a pillar of fire by night. Gripped by fear and rebellion, the Israelites were never permitted to see the Promised Land. However, the Lord allowed Caleb and Joshua to enter due to their faith.

> *But because my servant Caleb has a different spirit and follows me wholeheartedly, I will bring him into the land he went to, and his descendants will inherit it.*
> *Numbers 14:24*

When our Caleb was born, there were negative giants—the neurologist, the MRI, the CT scan, the doctor's report, the insurance company… But Caleb had a positive attitude. He endured years of therapy as a newborn, toddler, and young boy. As a child, he pushed through and cooperated with his therapists. He was dripping with sweat, but he wasn't complaining.

Just as the spies encountered difficulty, we, as parents, experienced many discouraging times of despair. The intensity was too much to bear. We didn't see an end in sight. However, in hindsight, we began to see how God was moving and making a way.

Caleb conquered lifting his head and sitting up.

He conquered turning over, army crawling, and standing.

He conquered sounds, syllables, words, and sentences.

Our Caleb has a servant's heart. He is a servant as the Mayor of Muttland Meadows; only a servant would want to pick up dog poop. He helps people everywhere he goes. If someone struggles with groceries, he carries the groceries, even though he is often shuffling along, unsteady, and unstable.

We see that different spirit in our Caleb. And we are also interpreting this diagnosis through the eyes of faith in our God. With Him, all things are possible!

Caleb the Conqueror!

The Diagnosis

Caleb was diagnosed with Agenesis of the Corpus Callosum, meaning the bridge between his brain's right and left sides never developed.

According to the National Organization for Disorders of the Corpus Callosum: "The corpus callosum is the largest connective pathway in the human brain. It is made up of more than 200 million nerve fibers that connect the left and right sides (hemispheres) of the brain. Each hemisphere of the brain is specialized to control movement and feeling in the opposite half of the body, and each hemisphere specializes in processing certain types of information (such as language or spatial patterns). Thus to coordinate movement or to think about complex information, the hemispheres must communicate with each other. The corpus callosum is the main connector that allows that communication. If the nerve fibers don't cross between the hemispheres during the critical prenatal time, they never will. Absent Corpus Callosum (ACC) becomes a permanent feature of the individual's brain."

Disorders of the Corpus Callosum include Complete and Partial ACC. Caleb has Complete Agenesis of the Corpus Callosum (ACC). The National Institute of Neurological Disorder and Stroke suggests, "It is estimated that at least one in 4,000 individuals has a disorder of the corpus callosum."

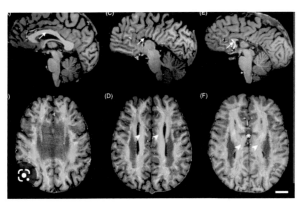

Left: normal corpus callosum.
Center: Complete ACC. Right: Partial ACC.

The symptoms and challenges related to ACC vary from mild to severe. As with many, the diagnosis is compounded with other issues and diagnoses.

He also has Colpocephaly— enlarged ventricles. As stated in the National Organization for Disorders of the Corpus Callosum, "Colpocephaly is a congenital brain abnormality in which the occipital horns— the posterior or rear portion of the lateral ventricles (cavities) of the brain—are larger than normal because white matter in the posterior cerebrum has failed to develop or thicken." The average ventricle size in the brain is 8-11 mm, in contrast to Caleb's, which is 28 mm.

By six years old, Caleb's other compounding diagnoses included Anxiety Disorder with Obsessive-Compulsive Disorder behaviors, Sleep Disturbance, ADHD–Inattentive type, Cognitive Delay, Speech and Language Disorder, Sensory Integration Dysfunction, Vision, Spasticity and Orthopedic Problems, and Psychosocial Stressors—upset by change and transitions.

Throughout our days at the hospital, we were utterly overwhelmed—medical jargon that was a foreign language to us, we did not know how we would pay the medical bills, and generally bewildered with the next steps. When the doctor stopped by early in the morning, I started with my first step, "Could you please write down the two diagnoses?" I could not remember their names, much less pronounce them.

"Agenesis of the Corpus Callosum and Colpocephaly," he said as he wrote them down.

In the quietness of the morning, my heart and soul cried out to God in pain and dismay.

Why did this happen?

What did I do during my pregnancy that caused this?

Was it from the tuna I was craving?

Was it from being exposed to a virus?

Feeling buried with anguish, I had to let these paralyzing thoughts go and surrender as the emotions continued to bombard me. Time and time again, there was a peace that passed all understanding and washed over me.

Bleak Report

The day after giving birth was emotional, as Andy, my parents, and I met with the neurologist. With a quick flip of his wrist, the neurologist clipped two black and white MRIs to the brightly lit screen in front of us, one of a healthy brain and one of Caleb's brain. It was gut-wrenching to literally see in black and white, Caleb's brain image in stark contrast with a healthy newborn brain. Without an ounce of empathy, the neurologist painted a bleak picture of Caleb's life, telling us that he would probably never walk or talk. The absent corpus callosum will affect his large motor skills, small motor skills, and speech. Among other things, he said Caleb would probably have seizures. I sat in the wheelchair, numb and speechless, as Andy and I tried to take in his cold and expressionless words.

He said, "I know you have questions, but I need to get back to my office."

Furious, my mom hurled back, "No, you are not. They have questions, and if they don't, I do!" I was thankful for my mamma bear stepping in because we had nothing to give but blank stares. As devastating as it was, God was present. The doctor stayed a few minutes longer and explained that extensive physical therapy could encourage brain growth due to our early detection.

The neurologist continued to see Caleb for years after that first encounter. In my flesh, I wanted to prove him wrong, but ultimately, I wanted him to see what God could do. Caleb continued to amaze him with his progress, especially his ability to connect and charm people. When emotions were not raw and heightened, I realized what was essential—a neurologist understands the brain, not feelings. But it's certainly a bonus if they have a reasonable bedside manner! After several visits, the neurologist made this analogy, "Caleb does not have the main highway in his brain, but he will take the back country roads to hopefully get there." God has designed the brain to make connections through therapy, play, repetition, and stimulation. We did everything we could to provide an environment conducive to brain development.

We were grateful for Caleb's diagnosis at birth because we could immediately begin his therapy. While in the Intensive Care Unit, we listened attentively as the physical therapist taught us exercises to lift his legs and stretch his fingers. It quickly became apparent this would be a very slow process with little assurance that change would happen. *How are these little leg lifts, bending his knees, and stretching his fingers going to do anything?* The first physical therapy session was the beginning of a very long faith journey, believing God was healing Caleb.

Following Caleb's first physical therapy session, while Andy and I were still processing that he may never walk or talk, the financial assistant ushered us into her office. She proceeded to rattle off details about resources, finances, medical jargon, and insurance. As we sat in a fog, the Charlie Brown teacher talk droned on. It wasn't the right time to bombard parents with this. I don't know when it is, but that was not the time. Our hearts were broken, and we could not take in any more information.

Jesse

A few days after Caleb was born, we met with another doctor in the hospital. He said the best thing we could do was have another baby close in age. It was a scary thought after the trauma we had just gone through; however, it made perfect sense to me. He believed Caleb's sibling would help him meet major milestones through watching and imitating. I was immediately on board, Andy not so much. Understandably, he was concerned and overwhelmed by the enormity of the challenge in front of us. As with many couples, God wired us differently. I knew getting pregnant with Caleb was a miracle. It would take another miracle to get pregnant again right away. We went to a genetic specialist to see if his brain disorder was genetic; she believed it was not.

By God's grace, I became pregnant with our second baby when Caleb was seven months old. We were ecstatic! Since Andy had to work, he was not with me during my first ultrasound. As the nurse proceeded with the ultrasound, she paused and asked, "Do you see what I'm seeing?"

I exclaimed, "Aw, there's the baby."

She nudged, "Look closer."

"Twins! I'm having twins!!" My emotional barometer skyrocketed! "This can't be" shifted to pure joy and excitement within seconds! I was over the moon! "How am I going to tell Andy?"

Two weeks later, we had another ultrasound. I will never forget when the nurse clicked away on the screen in the dark room. She very matter-of-factly stated, "There is only one baby in here now." I was shattered, Andy

was numb, and Caleb sat in his car seat, smiling from ear to ear. Everyone sitting in that small room experienced their own unique emotion. Within moments, God graciously transformed my devastation into gratitude for our remaining healthy baby I was carrying. The nurse explained "Vanishing Twin Syndrome," or VTS, is when one baby does not develop and is absorbed into the mother's system.

Due to Caleb's brain disorder, they closely monitored the baby's development. Months later, while undergoing a high-tech ultrasound with a specialist, I told him we were having twins at one time. To our amazement, we could see the other baby, who had never developed past the size of a pea. God, in His divine plan, took one baby home to be with Him. Years later, at a Steven Curtis Chapman concert, God laid it on my heart to name the baby, so Simon or Simone will be reunited with us in heaven.

On August 15, 2001, Jesse Hunter was born. Our prayers were answered, and our hearts were full as we praised God for our healthy baby boy.

A Match Made in Heaven

At 16 months apart, Caleb and Jesse were inseparable, affectionate, and true companions. Caleb adored Jesse and wanted to keep up with him. They used their imaginations as they played dress-up, organized cupboards, and rode their motorized jeeps. All of Caleb's therapy and early intervention were life-changing and taught Caleb many things, but Jesse was his best teacher.

It was evident that God designed them to be a perfect pair. They leaned on each other's strengths. Caleb shined in social settings, whereas Jesse struggled with social anxiety. Caleb would shuffle to the door with open arms when the doorbell rang, while Jesse would hide behind the couch. When Jesse felt comfortable, he ran to his room to get his guitar, then placed it at the guest's feet. He wanted to engage in conversation, but it did not come naturally.

Jesse, on the other hand, could navigate a new situation. With his independent nature and strong intellect, he could take the lead and figure things out when Caleb had difficulty getting around and did not always understand. This dynamic was evident at my parents' 50th wedding anniversary celebration, when Jesse confidently dismissed the guests to the serving line as Caleb welcomed and engaged with each

one. They have both grown from each other's example and character strengths.

Chapter Resources:

National Organization for Disorders of the Corpus Callosum
www.nodcc.org

National Institute of Neurological Disorders and Stroke
www.ninds.nih.gov

Early Intervention Is Key

Now faith is the substance of things hoped for,
the evidence of things not seen.

Hebrews 11:1

Birth to Three

We are grateful for Caleb's detection and diagnosis at birth because early intervention made all the difference for him. Knowing we needed to build pathways in his brain during his formative years, we put him in every available therapy to stimulate his brain, cross the mid-line, and create pathways.

Integrated Learning Strategies states, "The right side of your child's brain is used for creativity (coloring, art, music, drawing, imaginative play), and the left side of their brain is used for higher learning concepts (reading, writing, language, problem-solving, critical thinking). If the two sides of the brain are disconnected or if they are not wired to "talk" with each other, a child could struggle with learning challenges, speech and language delays, emotional grounding problems, attention and focus issues, and lack of communication.

Your child's corpus callosum is the "superhighway" of the brain that ultimately connects and wires your child's brain for higher academic performance. This is why it is a good idea to engage kids in crossing the mid-line activities. These types of exercises can rewire and engage both the body and the brain for reading, writing, spelling, speech, attention, and math."

We were blessed beyond measure with dedicated, caring, and exceptional therapists for the Birth to Three Program at Penfield Children's Center. Caleb's physical therapist, Julie Wellenstein, and I realized we went to high school together when she came on the first day of in-home physical therapy. Engaging a toddler in physical and speech therapy is a tedious process. It

can be depressing as a parent, so to have Julie and the speech therapist, Michele, share in our world, walk with me through difficult days, and celebrate the smallest victories filled my soul.

Even though Caleb could not speak with words, he spoke volumes with his bright eye contact, alertness, and engagement with people as they talked to him. At six months, he met my sister, Lynda, for the first time. As Lynda sweetly spoke to him, Caleb puckered his lips and carried on an engaging conversation with "Oooo." Everyone wanted to hold him because he was an expressive, happy baby who hardly ever fussed or cried.

Tried as we may, he could not say "Caleb," until one day, he uttered, "Babo!"—an endearing name indeed.

Trusting God with Our Finances

I will have no fear of bad news,
for my heart is steadfast, trusting in the Lord.

Psalm 112:7

As the astronomical hospital and therapy bills poured in, I begged for financial assistance. I cried with my mother, who always reminded me to trust Him. In her wisdom, she encouraged us to "expect a miracle and praise Him in advance," and He faithfully provided.

Our lack of money led to greater dependence on God. Many potential resources came through hunting, researching, and completing time-consuming applications. Some were denied, but I kept pressing on. Caleb did not qualify for much assistance when he was first born. For some agencies, his disability wasn't significant enough because he wasn't missing any milestones at a few months old. Other agencies recognized his significant disability, but we made slightly too much money. Yet, the bills and the need for early intervention were immediate. It was frustrating, but after persistence and countless phone calls, emails, and inquiries, in 2002, a miracle happened—Caleb qualified for Katie Beckett Medicaid.

Katie Beckett Medicaid is a "special eligibility process that allows certain children with disabilities or special health care needs to obtain health care coverage under Wisconsin's Medicaid Program." Eligibility is based on the child's needs rather than the parent's income. With Caleb's Medicaid card, many services were paid in full—physical therapy, occupational therapy, speech, prescriptions, doctor appointments, wheelchair expenses, and medical supplies.

Thankful, I embarked on my next leg of the journey to find the right therapists that accept Medicaid, wait for pre-approval, and appeal if denied. All of it required excessive piles and files of tedious applications and paperwork. Advocate, advocate, advocate! I pushed through my weariness and fought for Caleb. Early intervention is key, but being a tenacious advocate is just as crucial. I was relentless in searching for available services. Caleb is where he is today because we advocated for him to receive every resource we could find.

Hippotherapy

Hippotherapy (*hippo* is Greek for horse) was another impactful therapy for early intervention. According to the American Hippotherapy Association, "Hippotherapy refers to how occupational therapy, physical therapy, and

speech-language pathology professionals use evidence-based practice and clinical reasoning in the purposeful manipulation of equine movement as a therapy tool to engage sensory, neuromotor and cognitive systems to promote functional outcomes." Physical therapist Anne Roemke, who incorporates hippotherapy into her practice, was an incredible

advocate and godsend! Caleb didn't have the core muscle strength to sit up unassisted at two years old.

As I watched him propped on a giant horse, crouching forward and collapsing on himself, it was hard to comprehend how this could be helpful. As the horse started taking steps with Anne by his side, Caleb sat up straight, rolled his shoulders back, and smiled gleefully. Jesse and I ran through the pasture on that

sunny day as the horse slowly trotted with Caleb on his back. I was taking pictures like crazy, fully embracing this miraculous moment!

Move To Ozaukee County

When the boys were two and three years old, we lived in Milwaukee County, but we knew that neighboring Ozaukee County offered the most funding for special needs families. Knowing we couldn't afford that area, we prayed that God would provide, and once again, He did. In 2003, we bought a complete fixer-upper in charming Cedarburg, Wisconsin.

After researching funding sources, I knew we needed to get on the waiting list for Ozaukee County Children and Families immediately. Amid our move, with a cluttered mess and boxes stacked everywhere, I met with Howard Mulloy, the Family Services Specialist. Following the functional screening that evaluated his progress at three years old, Caleb was eligible for Children's Long Term Support Waiver Programs, which provide federal, state, and local funding for needed goods and services. We waited six years to get off the waiting list, but when he was nine years old, he received funding for respite care, daily living skills, and supportive home care services. We were grateful for the foresight to get the process in motion and the funding we received years later.

Therapy, Therapy, and More Therapy

Since Caleb had Medicaid, he could now receive services at Ozaukee Therapy. We met some of the most dedicated therapists who impacted our and his life. Since the boys were 16 months apart, Jesse went to every appointment with us. Those days were often grueling, as every day was filled with crushing thoughts and fears for his future. Since he couldn't walk, I had to carry him on my hip; Jesse was hyperactive, so he would motor in the opposite direction.

While attending occupational therapy (OT), physical therapy (PT), and speech and language therapy (SPL) was draining, it made an impactful difference. God's design of the brain is miraculous because it creates new pathways.

"Neuroplasticity is the brain's ability to reorganize itself by forming new neural connections throughout life. Neuroplasticity allows the neurons (nerve cells) in the brain to compensate for injury and disease and to adjust their activities in response to new situations or changes in their environment," as defined in MedicineNet.

In addition to OT, PT, and SPL, Caleb participated in Kindermusik, music therapy, swimming lessons, and aquatic therapy to stimulate his brain and cross his mid-line. He also did therapeutic listening. CORA Physical Therapy states, "Therapeutic listening is a sound-based intervention that was developed to support people of all ages who experience difficulties with sensory processing. It provides stimulation to the auditory system through the use of specifically altered music. This music is designed to stimulate the nervous system and the areas of the brain we use to listen and process sensory information." While he played quietly, he wore headphones, either listening to therapeutic listening CDs or classical music.

When Caleb was five years old, I was driving our minivan, looking in the mirror at the boys behind me in their car seats. Caleb exclaimed, "I see two mommies!" My heart sank because I realized that he was experiencing double vision. *No, God! Please, not this too!* After more research, the doctor confirmed our fear and recommended vision therapy—more therapy, more driving, and another commitment to add to our schedule. But we would do everything we could for his early intervention. Andy's mom, Grandma Johnson, graciously took Caleb to "pirate school." Through exercises and wearing his eye patch to strengthen his eye muscles, the problem was eventually corrected.

In addition to therapy, we saw doctors and psychiatrists with varying approaches to address Caleb's sensory issues and diet for constipation and leaky gut. We had success with pharmaceuticals, integrative medicine, and a holistic approach, but it all required balance, dedication, and commitment.

Barb Hypes—An Absolute Godsend

Caleb's physical therapist, Barb Hypes, had not worked with him very long when we realized she was an exceptional therapist. I broke down as Barb, the boys, and I sat on the therapy room floor with the boys eating dripping ice cream cones. I often put on a brave face but could not control my despair. As I sobbed, Barb grabbed Kleenex and explained that we were at a crossroads and had a decision to make. We could continue to work with therapists who did conventional therapy. They could get him up to walk by three years old, but he would probably have a lifetime of surgeries.

In contrast, we could work with her. Barb did unconventional therapy. Her approach was very different because she looked at his whole body. She often reminded us that his lack of muscle tone and awkward gait was not a foot problem but a brain problem. Even if we did extensive surgeries to correct his walking, the foot alignment problem would return due to the absent corpus callosum. We had a decision to make. If we chose to go with her, she would not get Caleb to walk independently until he was about nine years old, but chances are, he would walk as an adult and avoid many surgeries. By God's grace, what she proposed made sense to us, even though we didn't want to wait six more years for him to walk. We chose to go with Barb, and God used her in miraculous ways to teach Caleb how to walk independently at nine years old.

Barb modeled her therapy after Temple Grandin. Through perseverance and determination, Temple Grandin has lived with the challenges of autism. She has written several books about what she is experiencing in her keen observation of a cow's behavior. The movie, *Temple Grandin*, is fascinating and inspiring. Grandin's articulation

of her obsessiveness, perseverating thoughts, and sensory issues explains how Caleb's brain is wired, especially regarding dogs and his creative mind. All of Temple Grandin's understanding factored into Barb's therapeutic approach to restoring Caleb's physical and mental health.

Barb strongly advocated for Caleb and taught us to do the same. Before doctors were allowed to do a procedure, they needed to confer with Barb since she had an acute understanding of his physical and sensory needs. She explained, "Caleb's mind is in a constant state of chaos due to his absent corpus callosum, and our job is to keep his brain as calm as possible. Don't add to his stress. The longer his brain stays in a constant state of chaos, the worse it is for his brain." The phrase she used to describe Caleb as "consistently inconsistent" is the most valuable insight that rings true and one we pass on to this day.

Barb's Insightful Email

Following Caleb's physical therapy sessions, Barb Hypes often wrote thorough, valuable emails to help us understand and advocate for him.

- Caleb's neurological insult (no connection between the two sides of his brain) causes him to be consistently inconsistent in his responses and actions.

- His insult causes him to have a primary problem with communication of information which affects his sensory organization. His motor system is abnormal because it receives inconsistent and poorly organized input from the poorly organized sensory system. The sensory system communication telling the muscles the intensity, timing, direction, speed of the movement may go through one time and may forget to release the next. He is not being uncooperative, he is being consistently inconsistent.

- If Caleb is feeling organized and like himself, he is a kid who thrives on rigid rules. So if he isn't following the rules, it is not because he is trying to misbehave, it is because he is overwhelmed or confused. Once he crosses over into this chaos (which can happen between breaths on a bad day) he quickly falls apart and will misbehave. But he truly doesn't like himself when he does this, so if this isn't reinforced or he isn't pushed when it is clear he is getting stressed, he won't resort to the negative coping.

- If Caleb is feeling organized and like himself, he is a very easy going and cooperative person. When he is testy and asking tons of questions and off task, he is actually unorganized and doesn't know how to figure out what he is supposed to be doing. So, he is a master at getting the adult off task. We have to remind ourselves to be the adults and not follow him down this sticky path he has created that gets him out of having to perform something he can't seem to understand at the moment.

At the time, Barb told us that we would be advocates for Caleb for the rest of his life. I thought, *Of course…that won't be hard…* I didn't consider that it would be with every setting and stage of his life. It is constant and exhausting. Some situations are very uncomfortable. It was freeing to come to the realization that some people will never understand. I do not need to waste needless energy explaining Caleb if they don't want to receive it.

Barb was an innovative, creative therapist who used PVC piping to construct whatever necessary equipment to stretch, rotate, and work Caleb's muscles and movement. She incorporated Kinesio taping and electrodes to fire the right muscles and created "moon boot" platforms and poles to help him balance and take steps. She told us that when he learned to walk independently, she would retire and write a book about him. And that is what she did. Barb documented all her therapy with Caleb from 3 to 11 years old with notes, pictures, and videos. *Caleb Through The Years, Volumes One Through Four* by Barb Hypes is a physical therapy manual that captures Caleb's journey from creeping to walking independently.

We are forever grateful for Barb's gift of investment in Caleb, the peace that Andy and I had to trust her explicitly, and the detailed manuals and DVDs documenting his progression. Currently, Barb is a renowned speaker and

therapist who teaches other therapists the approach she used for Caleb to help other clients.

Barb thought outside the box, yet, her approach resonated with Andy and me. My style is relational, so I did what came naturally to me. I did not want to be in constant disciplinary mode because I could see that Caleb didn't respond favorably. My goal was not to "win" the power struggle. I tried to avoid a power struggle because it clearly unraveled him and escalated the situation. We always try to keep it positive and reward rather than punish. The strategy that we constantly use is to distract and redirect him. I had to learn to stop listening to the opinions of others and do what came naturally to me.

I love that Andy is on the front cover of this manual with Caleb. Andy was a stay-at-home dad for many years while I was teaching. I have always admired Andy's patience and selflessness. He sacrificially attended endless therapy appointments at a time when most men were climbing the ladder in the workforce, but the investment was worth more than any money in the bank. Andy and Caleb have an undeniable bond since Andy actively participated in many therapy appointments to see firsthand the miracle of Caleb learning to walk independently.

When Andy and I were working and couldn't take Caleb to his appointments, Andy's mom, Grandma Johnson, immersed herself in Caleb's therapy and learned from Barb. Her generous offering was valuable and gave her a glimpse into our challenges with Caleb.

Caleb Through The Years, Volume One Through Four captures Caleb's sheer determination and perseverance and Barb's expertise and tedious devotion. Our priceless treasure from Barb was a signed copy of her book with four DVDs of footage of her working with Caleb and a heartwarming message:

Laura, Andy, Karen, and Caleb,

Thanks for all the questions that created the need for me to articulate and describe hypotonia and motor disorganization. But, more than anything, thanks for trusting me and taking an unpaved path to help Caleb achieve maximum function and minimal pathology. Everyone should have the privilege of working and laughing with a child who is as much fun as Caleb.

Good Luck!
Barbara

Chapter Resources:

Integrated Learning Strategies
www.ilslearningcorner.com

Penfield Children's Center
www.penfieldchildren.org

Katie Beckett Medicaid
www.dhs.wisconsin.gov/kbp/index.htm

Hippotherapy
www.americanhippotherapyassociation.org

Ozaukee County Children and Families
www.co.ozaukee.wi.us/279/Children-Families
- Children's Long Term Support Waiver Programs
- Birth to Three Program

Rehab Resources (Ozaukee Therapy)
www.rehabresourcesinc.com/outpatient-clinics

MedicineNet
www.medicinenet.com/neuroplasticity/definition.htm

Kindermusik
www.kindermusik.com

Therapeutic Listening
www.coraphysicaltherapy.com/what-is-therapeutic-listening

Vision Therapy
www.thevisiontherapycenter.com

Caleb Through The Years, Volumes One Through Four
Barbara Hypes
www.clinicians-view.com/BookPreviews/CBK1Preview.pdf

Over the Edge

Weeping may tarry for the night, but joy comes with the morning.

Psalm 30:5

Holidays are a special time. My mom created cherished memories with her grandchildren as she would make appearances as Minnie Mouse and Santa Claus. Their looks of childlike wonder and curiosity are treasured moments.

As much as we enjoyed the holidays, as for many, they were stressful. During a Christmas gathering when the boys were three and four years old, I had a rather honest conversation about raising Caleb and Jesse with well-meaning family members. As much as I wanted to exchange ideas and take in what I heard about discipline, I knew their experience with raising children was not our reality. At one point in the conversation, we discussed a common difference in parenting styles. I told them Caleb and Jesse slept with us because they didn't want to stay in their beds. Sleep meant more to us than any rigid routine. I had tried letting Caleb cry himself to sleep, but it only wound him up. I cherished Jesse wanting to snuggle with me before falling asleep.

That evening, we said our polite goodbyes and got in the car. Fueled by my intense conversation regarding discipline styles, a switch flipped in me. Andy was oblivious that "Mount Vesuvius" was about to blow. Before he hit reverse, I screamed, "I don't care that it is Christmas...the boys are going to sleep in their own rooms tonight! Get the drill and put locks on the outside of their doors." Knowing that he could not talk any sense into me at that moment, Andy came up from the basement with his drill in hand and proceeded to lock the boys in their rooms. I didn't care if they cried all night long. I was not going to let them out of their rooms. Of course, many told me that, eventually, they would fall asleep. Their crying would knock them out, and they would fall asleep. Nope. Their screaming only escalated, but I didn't care. It was anything but a *Silent Night*! Andy knew to leave me alone, except to say that he would have to stay in a hotel that night, "Fine! Then go!"

He never did go to a hotel, but it was a Christmas night to remember! With the adrenaline spike, I put away every Christmas gift and cleaned the house thoroughly; all the while, Caleb and Jesse screamed blood-curdling screams through the wee hours of the morning.

The next night, I put both boys in their rooms. To this day, I can still picture Jesse pleading in his bed with crocodile tears, "No fuffy goor!!" which translated, "Don't shut the door!!" Many may believe, *you taught him...it was worth it...you showed him who was boss…* No, to this day, I regret doing this to Jesse, especially knowing his anxiety as a little child.

On the other hand, Caleb stayed by the door when we put him in his room and yelled, "Shut the door…and lock it!" Being locked in his room gave him a sense of security. For us, it provided a reprieve and a safe place for him.

I learned that every child is different, and what works for one does not necessarily work for another. Know your child and treat them accordingly, not equally. This was a lesson that carried over for many years to come. From then on, it was apparent that the boys would live very different lives. We could not use the same discipline or rewards for both boys. They were individuals who needed to be treated individually.

You Carried Me

I thank God every time I remember you. In all my prayers for all of you,
I always pray with joy because of your partnership in the gospel from the
first day until now, being confident of this, that He who began a good work
in you will carry it on to completion until the day of Christ Jesus.

Philippians 1:3-6

In 1998, before we had children, my dear sisters in Christ, Julie Loomis and Cathy Melan, and I pioneered Eastbrook Academy, a private school in Milwaukee. I loved being a part of the trailblazing effort. The bonds and friendships formed have been a continued source of strength, and I am forever grateful for these lifelong friendships.

I was the kindergarten teacher, fundraising coordinator, and daycare director in our first year. I poured my heart and soul into it. It was home away from home for me, and I loved it.

After Caleb was born, I continued to teach kindergarten and later taught art part-time. My friends at the school were amazingly supportive prayer partners and caring listeners. They stepped in as the hands and feet of Jesus and provided many laughs to lighten the load—especially during dark days.

Under painful circumstances, Andy was let go from a job when Caleb and Jesse were three and four years old. I had to return to work full time as a fourth grade teacher. I desperately wanted to be home to take care of the boys and take Caleb to all his therapy appointments, but I was now the breadwinner and the one carrying our health insurance.

God was faithful and provided us with the help and support we needed. He led me to a cashier at a teacher supply store the day before school started. Appalled, I was relaying my panic about how expensive daycare was, and I wasn't sure how our special needs son would do. She excitedly told me about Julie Howard, the best home daycare provider for her special needs son. I connected with Julie, and the next day, I dropped off the boys at her house. Julie was another godsend who naturally and lovingly cared for our boys.

Needed Confirmation

When Caleb was in kindergarten at Eastbrook Academy, it got to the point that we just couldn't carry him on our hips anymore. We tried throwing him over our shoulders and giving him piggyback rides, but he was getting too heavy; his legs practically dragged on the ground. I knew it was time to get a wheelchair, but I was struggling with the thought of it. It was emotional because it was the next visible thing to show people he was disabled. I also felt if we "gave in," we were confining him to a wheelchair

for the rest of his life. It was one more transition that we just needed to accept. We were unsure and needed confirmation. One day, I had to leave school early to go to the doctor. Sick, crying, and completely depleted, I was driving down the road I had taken for years, but on that day, at that time, God gave me the confirmation I needed. There were three wheelchairs for sale at the end of the driveway near the road! When do you ever see that? Thank you, Lord. He heard my prayer. It was time. He cared about my aching heart.

Driving to work in the morning was a difficult time during my day. As a teacher, I needed to be at devotions by 8 a.m. Needless to say, I often didn't feel very spiritual after the rat race to school, but it was just what I needed. We had a half-hour drive. Since Caleb hated to wear his seatbelt, it was a constant struggle with lots of crying and yelling. To distract him and keep peace and order in the car, we practiced math facts the entire way to school. Here's how the conversation went every day.

Me: "Caleb, what's 0+1?"

Caleb: "0."

Me: "No, **1**…Jesse, what's 7+8?"

Jesse: "15."

Me: "Great! Caleb, what's 0+**1**?"

Caleb: "0."

Me: "No, **1**…Jesse, what's 800+900?"

Jesse: "1700."

Me: "Great! Caleb, what's 0 + **1**!!"

Caleb: "2."

Me: "No, it's **1**…"

This went back and forth every morning. It required patience, but it was a fun way to practice. It took until middle school before Caleb ever understood addition and subtraction. I decided a calculator was a great tool for multiplication! On the other hand, Jesse memorized his math facts quickly because of this routine. In November, he made it into the Fantastic Facts Club, a significant accomplishment for a kindergartner.

When we arrived at school, I had to get the wheelchair out of the car...piece by piece, reassemble it, get both boys out of the car, get Caleb seated, and wheel him to the front door. Once inside the school, I had to guide Caleb slowly and steadily down each step because he didn't have the core muscle strength, and then I had to carry the wheelchair down the flight of stairs since there wasn't an elevator and reassemble it. At this time, Jesse was hyperactive. All he wanted to do was run, do karate chops, and wrestle. Some who watched me do this daily routine would ask, "Are you Wonder Woman?" I would say "No," but this was my life. What was I supposed to do? To this day, I look back and wonder how I did it all. All I can say is, *Thank you, Lord, for the strength You provided!*

Just For Giggles

We are grateful for the solid phonics background that both boys received at Eastbrook Academy. Caleb learned to read in kindergarten by sounding out the letters. One day while reading the Christmas story, he said that Mary and Joseph had onions (union).

CARRIED TO THE TABLE

Often stressed and exhausted, I listened to the song "Carried to the Table" by Leeland every day on my way to work. It touched me deep in my soul. I could not get enough of it. I played and replayed this song for weeks straight, often singing through the tears. I wasn't even sure why it ministered to me until I looked up 2 Samuel 9. Mephibosheth, son of Jonathan, was left lame after being dropped by a nurse who rescued him from being murdered. Eventually, King David called for any living relative of King Saul's to join him at his ancestral table to eat and fellowship with him and his family.

With Caleb's diagnosis, our hearts have grieved, been broken, and depleted. Still, hope, encouragement, and renewed strength come through prayer. Caleb is being carried to Jesus' ancestral table in His care and fellowship with the King. When we have nothing more to give, our family and friends carry us to the King's table to be cradled in His arms.

Like King David, we must show the kindness of God to others. We see how Caleb pours kindness as he goes about each day. In return, the kindness others show him blesses us everywhere we go. This journey has been grueling and exhausting, but He has carried us, and we have been swept away by His love.

Carried to the Table
by Leeland Mooring
lyrics based on 2 Samuel 9

Wounded and forsaken
I was shattered by the fall
Broken and forgotten
Feeling lost and all alone
Summoned by the King
Into the Master's courts
Lifted by the Savior
And cradled in His arms

I was carried to the table
Seated where I don't belong
Carried to the table
Swept away by His love
And I don't see my brokenness anymore
When I'm seated at the table of the Lord
I'm carried to the table
The table of the Lord

Fighting thoughts of fear
And wondering why He called my name
Am I good enough to share this cup
This world has left me lame
Even in my weakness
The Savior called my name
In His holy presence
I'm healed and unashamed

You carried me, my God
You carried me

Desperate Need for Sleep

Caleb loved to fall asleep with his head at the crack of his bedroom door and butt up in the air. He would call us for hours from under the crack of his door. Even though he wasn't necessarily upset, he wanted us to know he was there. I usually didn't mind because I was so thankful we had the lock on his door, and he wasn't coming out. He spent countless hours lining up his matchbox cars in an orderly, obsessive fashion while uttering, "Brrrmmm" and singing "Old MacDonald Had a Farm." Just when we sighed a sigh of relief that he finally fell asleep, he would faintly eke out, "E-I," pause,

pause, pause, "E-I," pause, pause, pause, "O." We slid a wrapped slice of cheese under the door when he cried and wanted to come out. He went from "waaaaa" to "fank-oo" (thank you) in seconds. This routine went on for many years. I didn't think he would ever stop sleeping by the door.

We tried many things to make his bed appealing, including a bed tent. As he got older, we removed his bed since he wasn't using it and created a spa-type atmosphere, complete with a hammock, brushing therapy, lavender, and quiet music. At eight years old, he was old enough for sleep meds to calm his active brain, so thankfully, he eventually slept in his bed.

Caleb wanted me to be with him every minute of every day, interacting and responding to his every question. My supportive family and friends would try to step in, but he wanted Mommy! Due to chronic fatigue and thyroid issues, not to mention cortisol levels that were off the charts, I was incredibly sleep-deprived. All I wanted to do was crawl in the corner of the garage to sleep. I knew I was in trouble when, even when he wasn't calling for me, I could still hear, "Mommy, Mommy, Mommy!"

My protective sister, Brenda, is forevermore trying to solve the latest challenge with Caleb. She encouraged me to set up Andy's camping cot in the pitch-dark cellar basement, equipped with earplugs, pillows, and blankets. It was the soundproof refuge and secret hideaway I needed in the bowels of the house to steal a 20-minute power nap.

To this day, Caleb hates when I take a nap. If I am too quiet, he will yell, "Mom, are you sleeping?" I have many different responses, "No, I'm meditating!" "I'm reclining!" "I'm contemplating!" Desperate times call for desperate creative responses!

An Angel Named Jack

If I ever felt I was entertaining an angel, this was the day. I was completely and utterly drained and depleted. I had nothing more to give. I could not hold my head up for one more hour; I had to put it down. I stopped at a park with the boys, hoping they would be able to entertain themselves. This was not a problem for Jesse, but it certainly was for Caleb. There were not any climbing or outdoor toys suitable for a disabled child. All I knew was that I needed to park and drop. I had to put my head down. Out of nowhere, a teenage boy whisked Caleb away in his wheelchair and played hide-and-seek with him, Jesse, and his sister. He barely asked if he could take him; I'm sure he just knew. Not only did he play with Caleb, but he also treated him as if he could run. With Caleb bouncing around in his wheelchair, laughing his guttural laugh, they swerved around pine trees in the sunshine. He gave legs to Caleb as only a teenage boy could as the sun and Son shone down on us! I sat back in awe of how God heard my cry and answered it simply, whimsically. Not only did it give me the needed rest, but it also filled my soul to the core. I sat on my blanket, crying at God's presence, goodness, and creativity. I got his name, Jack, as he quickly fluttered out of our lives.

Stressful Car Rides

Many parents can relate to stressful car rides. Being a captive, trapped audience with an obsessive child who didn't want to keep his seatbelt on and who didn't understand cause and effect, kept us on high alert. When Caleb obsessed about something, we needed to answer his question a million times, in a million different ways, creatively offering him whatever was available to keep him occupied. Scary, but one day when he was five years old, he was out of sorts and opened the car door while I was driving! Thankfully, I was able to pull over immediately. Sheer panic raged through me as Jesse leaped over Caleb to shut the car door the first time it happened. He calmed Caleb down and gently talked to him, even though his anxiety was through the roof.

During times like these, you recognize your life is not typical, and not many people can relate. You begin to believe the lies of judgmental people who think they could do a better job of raising him. "You just need more discipline," or, "Caleb is controlling and manipulating you." It is infuriating to wrestle with these thoughts when we know we have exhausted every possible scenario. We have researched, prayed, tried every discipline technique, and bought every car safety contraption. As he got older, he would still threaten to do it. His arms were long enough to put the window down, reach over, and open it from the outside. What worked one time may not work the next. He did not understand the grave consequence of opening a car door. We needed to help him understand.

In an effort to make an impact on Caleb's brain and help him turn a corner regarding unbuckling his seatbelt, I took the boys to the police station so that a police officer could talk to him about seatbelt safety. I didn't call beforehand, so I wasn't sure how the officers would respond, but they were happy to help. Before we went in, I told Jesse, who was deathly afraid of not wearing his seatbelt, that this conversation was not for him. Both boys sat at attention on the bench while the officer drove his point home. Jesse whispered in my ear, "If this is not for me, why is he looking right at me?" Sweet boy. Little did

Jesse know at the time, but these unique situations built character in him… tolerance, understanding, flexibility, and compassion. Having the "rule" come from the source was impactful. Caleb wore his seatbelt and didn't obsess about it as much anymore.

As Caleb got older, we always needed to be proactive and stay one step ahead of him. One day he was having a meltdown; he grabbed the steering wheel while I was driving. If he sat in the back seat, he would come from behind and reach over my shoulder when driving. It happened a handful of times, but enough to freak us out. Of course, we pulled over and didn't drive when Caleb was in that frame of mind. We tried many strategies and remained flexible and creative to prevent chaos from erupting:

- Avoid having him in a car when he is upset
- Rearrange driving situations ensuring he is content; maybe drive separately or let him sit by the window
- Provide him with every electronic device possible
- Interact and count trucks to pass the time
- Play the music he wanted, even if it meant listening to SCAN for 30 minutes
- Allow him to call friends and family
- Pretend things didn't bother us
  - Let him blast the heat. Eventually, he would get hot and turn it down
  - Let him roll down the window in the dead of winter. Eventually, he would freeze and roll it back up

Change in Routine

Caleb had a difficult time with a change in his routine. Taking him out of school for any reason, especially doctor appointments, was challenging. Occasionally it helped to give him a warning, but some days it made it worse. One day when he was in high school, he needed to get to his early morning psychiatrist appointment. He was so upset when I turned left that he grabbed the steering wheel to turn right because that was the way to school. We had to crawl to the psychiatrist's office because every time he came close to touching the steering wheel, we pulled over. Late and frazzled, I begged the psychiatrist for answers to handle the situation. I answered my question, "I should have turned right and headed towards the school and kept talking about the reward he would receive after the appointment. This would allow more time for him to adjust his thinking, right?" He said, "Yes, that is exactly right." I knew it!

I didn't want to be late, but that strategy usually worked for Caleb. Next time I needed to allow more time for the creative route!

Adjusting Our Vacations

We have many cherished family memories while visiting Grandma Sandy and Grandpa "Up North" when the boys were little. However, there came a time when traveling with the boys became too difficult. Between red alert

car rides, Caleb's obsessiveness, sleeping disorders, and differences in mobility, vacations as a family were not working anymore.

Still wanting Jesse to experience childhood vacations, Jesse and I made memories at the waterparks. My girlfriend and I relaxed on the lazy river as Jesse and his friend had fun.

When the boys were in high school, we revisited having family vacations in Door County, Wisconsin, with Aunt Jane. She understood our challenge and graciously met our needs by driving short twenty-minute jaunts of go-karting for Caleb and shopping for Jesse. God answered my prayer beyond my expectations as Jesse was invited to go on three Caribbean vacations with family and friends. Thankfully, we can vacation and have fun together as a family again now that Caleb is a young man.

Mommy, You're Stupid

When Caleb was six years old, I experienced his relentless obsession directed at me. He was obsessed with saying, "Mommy, you're stupid." My initial reaction was obviously, *How inappropriate! Who says that to their mother!* I told him to stop, but it had no effect. I disciplined him, took away privileges, addressed it every time he said it, ignored it, and did not take it personally. It had no effect. I tried to explain his obsessiveness to others who heard it; that frustrated me as well. I came across as a softie, making excuses for him, and defensive as they implied that if only "they" could work with him, "they" wouldn't allow it. Once again, this judgmental, often unspoken, yet loud and clear response from friends, relatives, and strangers exasperated me. This obsession continued for days, weeks, months, and for what seemed like decades. I needed it to stop because I was losing my mind over it. I knew Caleb loved me more than life, but he didn't seem to understand its severe impact on me.

In total and complete desperation, I called his physical therapist, Barb, at home, sobbing as I was curled up on our steps, "He won't stop… 'Mommy, you're stupid.' I don't know what to do, and I am about to lose my mind!" As always, she encouraged me and explained that he had a short in his circuit, and I was caught in his obsessive loop.

There was no breakthrough until, finally, when we had friends over one evening and Caleb had to go to the bathroom. As he sat on the toilet, I knelt close to him, and he whispered, "That guy is stupid."

"What guy?" I whispered.

"That guy downstairs," he responded.

Knowing he loved our friend, I couldn't understand why he said that. But the Holy Spirit swept in and enlightened me to whisper, "Caleb, what does stupid mean to you?" He whispered back, "mean."

OH, MY! A breakthrough! My Helen Keller Moment! The heavens opened! I understood!

I'm not stupid; I'm mean! I have never been so delighted to be mean.

At that moment, it all made perfect sense. Caleb thought that our friend was mean when he was disciplining his child. He thought I was mean because I made Jesse go to his room when he needed discipline. He thought I was being mean to him because rather than carrying him on my hip, I was making him walk more on his own. I was in the thick of correcting behavior. He sensed my change and didn't know how to articulate it.

Once I had that breakthrough with him on the bathroom floor, he never called me stupid again.

Whenever Caleb is in an obsessive pattern, I am reminded and encouraged that the obsession will eventually pass. It is often a matter of finding the correct word, phrase, or experience that will resonate with him and help him turn a corner. It is fascinating and overwhelming to think, for Caleb, the meanings of words may not be what they actually mean. He may not know the connotations and denotations of some words…*but which words?*

Which Words?

At six years old, Caleb obsessively asked, "Mommy, do I need you? Do I need you, Mommy?" He didn't ask anyone else, just me. One day when he was going on a new outing, he asked, "Mommy, do I need you? Do I need you, Mommy? I responded, "Caleb, what does *need* mean to you?" He spelled, I'm s-k-a-r-e-d. "You're scared?" He said,

"Yes." I think he got nervous and just wanted that security. He uses some words that mean one thing to us but entirely something else to him. Once his understanding of the word was solved, I could address his nervousness and talk it through with him.

```````````````````````````````````````````````````````````````````````````````````

At 23 years old, Caleb still hates to shower. We always told him he didn't want to smell like pee or urine. No matter how we worded it, it didn't bother him. But one day, I told him he didn't want to smell like a urinal. Now that he could understand! It never dawned on me that he could associate that tangible stink of a urinal rather than urine.

## Chapter Resource:

"Carried to the Table"
Leeland Mooring - Sound of Melodies
www.youtube.com/watch?v=6jjpK7Kn2IM
```````````````````````````````````````````````````````````````````````````````````

Stepping Out in Faith

*May the God of hope fill you with all joy and peace as you trust in Him,
so that you may overflow with hope by the power of the Holy Spirit.*

Romans 15:13

During my tenth year at Eastbrook Academy as the Middle School Head, I began to feel that my time there was coming to an end. *But how could I quit? Would we make it without my income and insurance coverage?* I was emotionally and physically spent by the time I got home, so I had nothing to give to my own family. The Lord made it abundantly clear through various circumstances that I needed to take a leap of faith and quit my job without another job in sight. I was thankful for the incredible experience and grateful for the lifelong friendships, but I just couldn't do it anymore. As painful and stressful as it was, Andy and I had to walk away from Eastbrook, which was everything familiar, comfortable, and where we first began as a couple.

As I embarked on the unknown, I applied for an art substitute position at a different private school, University School of Milwaukee. On the morning of the interview, I was at peace as I walked on the winding sidewalk of their stunning campus. I was so taken by the beauty of the flowers and the friendly people. I knew I had a strong resumé with my elementary and special education degree, teaching and administrative experience, and reading license. Still, it was apparent during the interview that I didn't have the art experience needed for this position. However, little did I know my resumé was circulating. An administrator interrupted the interview to say that the Learning Center Coordinator would like to speak with me. As I stepped into the doorway of her office, she said, "Laura Griswold, you are such an answer to prayer. You have the job!"

In total shock, I replied, "Really? Great! What will I be doing?"

She explained that I would be a learning specialist, tutoring 1:1 in a private office. I knew it was an absolute fit at that time in my career. My position uses my strengths of building relationships, advocating, and assisting struggling students to strengthen their academic and executive functioning skills while providing support for parents. My new job at USM in 2008 was answered prayer for both of us!

Elementary Years

*Teach me Your way, Lord, that I may rely on Your faithfulness; give me an
undivided heart, that I may fear Your name.*
Psalm 86:11

Everything was going so well when the boys started their new elementary school. Jesse wheeled Caleb a block down the street to the sweet crossing guard, Vic. Life, for one brief moment, was so easy!

One day the school called to ask why Caleb was absent. I had sent him! *Where was he?* Panicking, we began the search only to find him as calm and happy as could be, watching the maintenance man cut the grass. He was mesmerized by the monotonous motion...back and forth.

Caleb had many caring teachers in elementary school. One exceptional teacher's aide has a son on the autism spectrum, so she understood. At the time, he hated to go to the bathroom. Many aides tried to get him to move, but she figured out what motivated him and made it into a game. She had a piece of paper hanging in the bathroom. Every morning, she went into the bathroom, wrote down the name of someone he knew and loved, and then left the note for him to see. She wrote down Mickey Mouse, Donald Duck, and Scooby... Every day, Caleb was eager to see who was in the bathroom. It was a simple game that made it fun and diffused the power struggle. I have used that strategy in various forms throughout his life.

LeRoy Butler

In 2010, Caleb, Jesse, and I walked toward the store in Sendick's parking lot. As Caleb hobbled along using his walking sticks, Hall of Fame football player LeRoy Butler came running towards us. He encouraged Caleb to keep going in his efforts to walk, and he shared his inspirational story. He was born pigeon-toed, and the doctors needed to break bones in both feet to correct it. He wore leg braces and used a wheelchair until he was eight years old. I was awestruck at what was happening, but, of all days, I didn't have my phone to take a picture. Since Butler was warm and personable, I asked if we could capture this special memory on his camera. As they posed for

the photo, Butler didn't realize that Jesse was standing behind him, and he accidentally stood on Jesse's foot. Imagine the weight of an NFL player on his nine-year-old foot! Needless to say, we were overjoyed with this encounter, but it took Jesse a while longer to be a Packer fan.

Jesse was absolutely my go-to man. Even though he was in elementary school himself, I depended on him for support with Caleb. There were numerous daily situations in which Jesse had to take the lead as an adult because Caleb was having a meltdown, or I couldn't take him inside a building because we couldn't use the steps. I remember needing to check out of the Grand Geneva, a lovely hotel, but I knew I could not physically do it. I sent Jesse off to check out at the front desk. As he walked down the sidewalk with my wallet bulging in his back pocket, it brought tears to my eyes. I knew he could barely see over the counter, but I needed him to step into an adult situation once again.

Andy was an amazing help, but he was often at work when the boys were little. I could not raise Caleb without Jesse stepping up and taking on a huge responsibility. Unintentionally, and yet necessary, Jesse was forced to grow up so much faster than most kids his age. I would not have been able to attend to Caleb's demanding needs without Jesse's patience, selflessness, and sacrificial love.

Safe Haven

Living with Caleb was not easy for us as parents and certainly not for Jesse as a brother. He witnessed the same meltdowns, chaos, and crazy compromises we made to keep him happy. Like many pre-teens, Jesse did not want to draw attention to himself and hated being embarrassed. On the other hand, Caleb often drew attention, so this stretched Jesse. It actually may have helped Jesse to be less self-conscious because if Caleb was doing something embarrassing, I tried to help him see the humor in it.

We realized that Jesse needed his own space, a place where he was free to be himself without the chaos, uncertainty, and responsibility of Caleb. This place was Skateland, the roller skating rink near our house. Skateland was Jesse's safe haven. He spent hours upon hours there. We assured him that this was his own space. When Jesse started roller hockey at 12 years old, we promised him we would not bring Caleb until he wanted him there. After a while, Jesse gave the okay for Caleb to go to his games. Doing something as a family was fun, and Caleb was his biggest cheerleader. Caleb quickly made his presence known, and the coaches asked him to be the scorekeeper, hand out treats, and even play goalie on Family Night. Jesse shined at hockey, and we were happy to see him excel.

A Dark Place

*My flesh and my heart may fail, but God is the
strength of my heart and my portions forever.*

Psalm 73:26

As the years continued, dropping Caleb off at school was difficult—another transition. He didn't want to be rushed. It was always helpful if I was not part of the process. A paraprofessional on car-line duty continued to open the door and let him out. One morning when I pulled up, she said, "I was told I couldn't open the door anymore for Caleb."

"Excuse me?" I questioned as the steam was coming out of my ears… I choked back tears and tuned out any explanation given to me. *You obviously don't have a clue as to how hard this is! I am not being lazy or demanding. Caleb responds faster when someone else triggers "get up and go." Is opening his door such an inconvenience?*

It was an ordinary, routine drop-off that hit a nerve when I was already at my breaking point.

For whatever reason, that episode sent me to a dark place. Delirious, I drove aimlessly around the subdivision, swearing, screaming at God, screaming at the para, and crying hysterically. The pent-up emotion exploded.

With its raw emotion, my broken heart reached its breaking point, and sadly, I took it out on the para that day. It was exhausting to be Caleb's advocate Every. Single. Day.

Officer Jake and Molly

*Fear not, for I am with you; be not dismayed, for I am
your God; I will strengthen you, I will help you. I will
uphold you with My righteous right hand.*

Isaiah 41:10

When the boys were nine and ten, we experienced a parent's worst nightmare. We knew Caleb went to school with a bruise on his side that day. We believed it was from a fall while sledding, but we didn't think much of it. I was home that day when suddenly a knock was at our door. There stood Officer Jake and social worker Molly from Social Services. *Now what? This can't be good news.* They explained that Caleb told an adult that his dad had hit him, and he showed them a bruise.

Terrified. *Are they going to take our children away from us?*

Angry. *Do they really think we are abusing Caleb?*

Panic. *What does our future hold? This will not be the first or last time Caleb will have an unexplained bruise... He is an open book and will say things that may only have a kernel of truth...*

Officer Jake and Molly were compassionate and understanding as we discussed Caleb's physical unsteadiness, meltdowns, and language deficiencies. I didn't feel they were accusing us of abusing Caleb, but they needed to follow up with what had transpired. As a teacher and former administrator, I am fully aware that we are mandated reporters and that the school was following the law. Nevertheless, it rattled me to the core.

Flooded by many emotions, I called our Family Service Specialist and explained that this would be our life… Caleb falls and runs into things all the time. He assured me that the last thing Social Services wanted to do was take away our children. He suggested I call Social Services. Talking to them took the fear out of it and put my heart at ease. Their suggestion was to meet with the school and talk it through. While the meeting was difficult, it was necessary for moving forward.

As a result of meeting Officer Jake and Molly, Caleb wanted to talk to his new friends, so he would call 911. His 911 obsession lasted for several years, which seemed like several decades! He called 911 on a very regular basis. Any time of the day, he would hold the phone and dial 9-1, and we would dive for the phone as he dialed the last 1. This crazy obsession was maddening for everyone. He did it…again! The police came...again.

Setting Boundaries

I waited patiently for the Lord; He turned to me and heard my cry.
He lifted me out of the slimy pit, out of the mud and mire;
He set my feet on a rock and gave me a firm place to stand.

Psalm 40:1-2

By this time in my life, I was completely depleted. I was sinking, exhausted, and couldn't muster the energy to care for one more thing. My life was a tangled mess, and I didn't know how to unravel it. I was so far gone in caring for others that I had lost myself.

Caleb needed me.

Jesse needed me.

Andy needed me.

Sherwood, the rambunctious dog, needed me.

Our marriage was crumbling. Our finances were sinking. My cortisol levels were through the roof. The messy house closed in on me. And, of all things, the pigsty of a garage got on my very last nerve. I hit rock bottom. Andy struggled with depression and undiagnosed Attention Deficit Disorder (ADD) but would not get help. He lost several jobs because of an inability to focus and multitask. We were not partners in our relationship; Andy had nothing to give either. He was just as depleted as I was. He was good to me, and I knew he loved me. He had the patience of a saint. How many men have the patience to be a part of this relentless chaos? It is no surprise that the divorce rate for families with a special needs child is high. We were drowning and didn't know how to pull ourselves out.

Since my well was empty, I was at a loss as to how to sort things out and too tired to chase after them, but I knew I needed to bring order and set boundaries for my sanity. I needed to identify the stressors and make changes to reduce the stress.

Identifying the stressors started with Sherwood, the dog. We needed to find a new home for our beagle shepherd mix puppy. As cute as he was, he was adding too much stress. Sherwood was not a naughty dog, but we could not give him the training he deserved. Thankfully, we found a loving home on a farm for Sherwood.

Over the next few months, my mission was to simplify, declutter, and practice self-care. It was empowering and invigorating, as I did the following:

- Met with a financial planner
- Hired a cleaning lady
- Joined a gym
- Worked with a nutritionist
- Subscribed for a meal delivery service
- Ordered groceries online and had them delivered to our house
- Went to counseling for myself
- Cleaned the garage
- Decluttered the house and took donations to Goodwill
- Sold things for money
- Returned things for money
- Drove metal and recycling to Waste Management
- Pampered myself by getting my nails done at the salon
- Enjoyed coffee with girlfriends often
- Visited my parents by myself in Arizona

PIPPI LONGSTOCKING

As a child growing up, my family ate dinner together every night. We always prayed together first, and the TV was never on. It is a special memory for me because every night, after my sisters and dad ate and left the table, my mom and I sat and talked for hours, pouring our hearts out to each other; actually, I poured my heart out to her. With her godly wisdom, she always pointed me to the Lord. When Andy and I started raising the boys, we went through so many dinners that needed to be less chaotic. I decided to read to them during dinner. I read *Pippi Longstocking*. It was a book I loved as a child. I don't even know if the boys were listening or understanding, but it was therapeutic for me to read a childhood book—we could be together without the chaos. The monotonous drone seemed to calm them.

Hope Does Not Disappoint

*We rejoice in our sufferings because we know that suffering produces
perseverance; perseverance, character; and character, hope.
And hope does not disappoint us because God has poured out His love
into our hearts by the Holy Spirit whom He has given us.*

Romans 5:3-5

Layer by layer, the tight, tangled mess began to loosen, and I had more hope. God gave me tremendous clarity, energy, and determination. Slowly but surely, things fell into place. Doors were opening. Healing was taking place. By the grace of God and my relationship with Him, I had hope again. I experienced a peace that only comes from God. He had not forgotten about me. He was taking care of me.

There was an exchange in my heart and soul:

- Pent up emotions to release
- Hopeless to hope
- Drudgery to living
- Darkness to sunshine
- Overwhelmed to overjoyed

Building Independence

*He will cover you with His feathers, and under His wings you
will find refuge; His faithfulness will be your shield and rampart.*
Psalm 91:4

The day I bought our family pool pass and reclined in the sun was a glorious day. Normalcy! We were doing what other normal people did on sunny days! Spending $180 was a lot for us, yet, I immediately knew it was the best money I had ever spent! I praised the Lord as I reveled in my newfound freedom, relaxing in the sun!

The boys were happy to swim in the pool where they had taken lessons, and I had comfort knowing that the lifeguards knew the boys. Caleb had to wheel through the men's bathroom, and hopefully, he'd find his way to the pool area. It was a small thing, but one of the first times that I was at the mercy of others to help if needed. Being a social butterfly, he made many new friends in the men's bathroom, and they often walked away with a smile because Caleb had a comment for everyone. It was apparent that many kind people were willing to lend a hand. Caleb hated to take showers, so eventually, I had him take showers at the pool, which was ideal for ease and building his independence. I didn't rush him because I was happy to wait by the pool; I was available if needed.

Some people disagreed with our approach to parenting. Some felt that we were relying on others to raise Caleb. Rumor had it that an unidentified peeping tom was at the pool for a while. I recognized that many things could go wrong, but I could not live in fear for the rest of my life. I needed to let go and let Him cover the boys with His feathers under His wings. We would do everything in our power to protect Caleb, but there was no way that we could be with him 24 hours a day. I knew the Lord would take better care of him than we possibly could. We needed to teach him to advocate for himself, navigate life, and become independent. The summer at the pool began my quest to find safe environments where I could teach him to build independence.

Caleb, Jesse, and I continued to go to the pool for many summers together. I could see Caleb had built many friendships with regular pool attendees and lifeguards. They greeted each other by name as he made his way around. He spent the entire afternoon swimming, playing in the sandbox, getting a snack, and talking to people. The beauty of the pool is that it is all enclosed. Caleb could not easily escape past the lifeguards on duty. When he was about 12 years old, I would leave for short periods after seeing he could manage without my being there the entire time. I extended the time the more I could see he could handle my absence. Eventually, I dropped him off, and he called me from the pool phone when he was ready to be picked up. As a result, his maturity and responsibility grew.

I maintained my sanity by taking a break from Caleb. It may have only been for an hour, but it made a huge difference. I sent the boys to the library, the bowling alley, the YMCA, and the Boys and Girls Club—just to name a few. I sent them to every Vacation Bible School I found, even if we didn't attend their church. I used to give them a quarter and let them ride their bikes to the rummage sales in the neighborhood.

In elementary school, the boys participated in many local recreation department activities. Jesse was on the swim team. I found out later that he hated it, but the swim team provided a lot of ribbons and praise for Jesse. It was a wonderful outlet, a place to work off a lot of energy and shine. Caleb loved attending swim meets and making new friends while sitting on the bleachers. At one swim meet, Caleb looked at a heavier-set woman and asked, "Do you jog?"

With a strange look, she responded, "Do I look like I jog?"

He replied, "No!"

We never know what is going to come out of his mouth.

Jesse also played basketball for the recreation department when he was nine years old. On his first day, Andy and I wheeled Caleb in his wheelchair to watch Jesse play. Shortly after it started, Coach Lenny came over, asked why Caleb wasn't playing and offered to work with him on basketball skills. Coach Lenny blew the whistle and gathered the team. Jokingly, he announced, "We have someone new on our team. Meet George." Jesse quickly responded, "He's not George. He's my brother!"

Coach Lenny's kind gesture began Caleb and Jesse's involvement at his JCC Rainbow Day Camp—an inclusive summer camp packed with entertainment, while I enjoyed needed "me" time!

The summer school class they took that still makes me chuckle was the coveted Titanic-themed adventure. On the first day, everyone was supposed to dress in character. Jesse and Caleb wore rolled-up jeans and suspenders, but we didn't have any caps for them to wear. When I dropped them off, the teacher was busy talking with students. I saw caps on the table and assumed they were there for those who didn't bring one, so I put one on Caleb and told Jesse to do the same. Jesse shook his head "no" with big eyes, not wanting to draw attention to himself. I wanted as much time to myself as possible, so I left without giving the teacher special instructions regarding Caleb. When the class started, the teacher, staying in character, walked to Caleb and rapped a ruler on his desk, scolding him for "stealing" the hat. Unaware of what was happening, Caleb repeatedly asked, "Why?" Again in character, she scolded him for being disrespectful. Jesse died a thousand deaths and was so thankful he didn't listen to me!

Looking back, those early years of allowing them to explore and have adventures on their own built self-esteem and independence that has carried over into their young adult years. Both boys welcome new experiences, take initiative, and problem-solve.

Divine Appointment

By divine appointment, God led me to Danielle in 2012. She was a stranger, but we immediately bonded when I entered her rummage sale. As I picked up a book, she burst with excitement, "I was just diagnosed with ADHD. I can now see the world in color. You have to read that book!"

"I know," I agreed. "But it is for my husband; he won't read it."

She enthusiastically replied, "Well, I need to talk to him."

To my surprise, Andy agreed to meet with Danielle. She spoke his language and convinced him to go in for an evaluation. He was diagnosed and went on medication for ADD. It was the beginning of Andy focusing better and feeling more alive.

While Danielle and I were bonding that day, Caleb and Jesse connected with Danielle's calm golden retriever, Sadie. I could see how the mellow dog brought calmness to the boys, and I craved calm. The connection we shared with Danielle and Sadie was a timely miracle that day, as the boys began dogsitting for Sadie, who quickly became part of our family.

Danielle eagerly supported Caleb's love for hair and beauty. She contacted Paul Mitchell Beauty School and arranged for Caleb to receive two mannequin heads. This began his mannequin head collection. He loved to play with the hair on his mannequin heads. One morning while showering, my heart skipped a beat to see four mannequin heads on the shower shelves staring back at me! We are thankful that God allowed our paths to cross with Danielle that summer day.

Fast Friends

After I intentionally simplified my life and schedule, the most significant trait I learned was contentment. Caleb moves at his own pace. He lives in the moment and experiences endless joy. Watching him navigate life taught me to slow my life down so I didn't miss the blessing.

Part of living in the moment is connecting with people. He observes and strikes up conversations with strangers, making them feel noticed and special, and people respond to him. One sweet memory was with Mary Jo Wirth when Caleb was 12 years old.

I dropped Caleb off at the entrance of Sendik's grocery store. As he shuffled to the electric carts, arms flailing to keep his balance, Mary Jo told him his shoe was untied. He inquired why she needed the electric cart. By the time I entered the store, they had become fast friends, laughing as they tootled around having electric cart races and gathering her groceries. Mary Jo and Caleb have remained friends to this day. She invited him to the nursing home for sing-alongs, surprised us by attending his graduation party, and supported his eventual dog portrait and art endeavors.

Chapter Resource:
JCC Rainbow Day Camp
www.jccmilwaukee.org/programs/camps/jcc-day-camps/day-camp

Everyone Needs a Kiki

Come to Me, all you who are weary and burdened, and I will give you rest. Take My yoke upon you and learn from Me, for I am gentle and humble in heart, and you will find rest for your souls.

Matthew 11:28-29

We had wonderful and supportive friends, but our social lives were impacted because caring for Caleb was always a factor. Sometimes only one of us could go. *Who was going to stay home with Caleb? Who was going to be able to handle him? If we brought him along, would he be content?* We couldn't be gone too long or far away if we suddenly needed to leave and tend to Caleb. However, for our mental health and the health of our marriage, Andy and I desperately needed a break to relax and go on date nights by ourselves and with friends.

We added respite care to Caleb's plan through the Children's Long Term Support Waiver. Budgeting this into his plan allowed us to get away for several hours a week. Sometimes parents feel guilty or don't see the need for respite care, but it was the best use of Caleb's funding when Jesse was 11 and Caleb was 12 years old.

Kiki left her business in California to spend more time with her elderly mother in Wisconsin. She had a natural passion for working with special needs children, so our lives changed when we met Kiki. She was not just a nanny; she was an extension of me. She came every morning at 5:30 a.m. to get Caleb ready and on the bus so that I could get ready for work. Our friendship was deep and intimate as we shared our hearts over coffee before the break of dawn. I could problem-solve with her because she was just as invested. Being a mother of a special needs child is often isolating, but God

quenched my desire for someone to "understand" when He brought Kiki into my life. She saw the underbelly of our family life and understood the depth of the challenge. It was intense and unrelenting when Caleb was in a bad place. I trusted her implicitly and could count on her to care for Caleb and Jesse just as she would her own family. Her intuition, judgment, and observations of the boys were spot on.

Kiki believed I was gifted in working with Caleb and soaked in everything that I was teaching her. She learned from my example how to navigate life with him and divert, distract, and redirect his obsessions. She treated Caleb and Jesse with great respect and related to them both as unique individuals. Jesse's motivation was food, so they would bond over their trips to Taco Bell and Skateland. She relied on Jesse when Caleb was melting down because he had the special touch to calm him.

During the summer months, Kiki watched Caleb for hours on end. Our goal was always to find fun, meaningful activities that would allow him to be independent yet supervised. Our answer to prayer was Muttland Meadows, a seven-acre enclosed dog park near our house. Kiki knew how much he loved dogs. She parked her car at the gate and allowed Caleb to go into the dog park to play with the dogs while she watched him from her car. Caleb was in dog heaven. He quickly noticed that the dogs were hot and needed fresh water in the empty dog dishes. His time with Kiki and his mission to fill the water bowls at Muttland Meadows was just the beginning! Years later, it became his home away from home.

An Incredible Ministry Team

At 12 years old, Kiki and Caleb spent the day with Carrie, a four-year-old nonverbal girl with autism. She noticed that Caleb had a sensitivity and a way of connecting with Carrie and getting her to interact. Kiki would often tell us about it, but we saw it for the first time when Carrie visited. The minute Caleb started playing the piano, she went by him and started touching him and wanting to be close, even though she usually didn't let people get close to her. She let him put her shoes on and tie them as she kept saying, "Ca-ub, Ca-ub, Ca-ub."

Kiki brought another young, nonverbal autistic friend, Shelby, into his life during that same time. They connected and began interacting together. Shelby carried a little recorder with her at all times. Clinging tightly to her recorder, Shelby didn't allow anyone to touch it. One day as Kiki was driving with Caleb in the front seat, Shelby tapped Caleb on the shoulder and handed him her recorder. A huge breakthrough! She was allowing Caleb into her world. Shelby had long, straight hair. Caleb, obsessed with mannequin heads, now had an opportunity to brush someone's natural hair who loved it. When her mom shared with Kiki about the noticeable changes she had seen in her daughter, Kiki mentioned that Caleb was brushing her hair. She was shocked because Shelby didn't let anyone get close to her and certainly didn't let anyone brush her hair.

Caleb's obsession with setting new ringtones on the phone drove him to set alarms that went off at odd times. One day an alarm sounded while

Shelby was at our house. Everyone in the room scrambled while laughing and screaming until they found the hidden phone. The next morning her mother cried as she told Kiki that her little girl talked! Not only did she speak, she told a story. Shelby's teacher called her mom, asking, "Who are Ca-ub and Kiki? We have never heard her talk this much before, and she is trying to tell us a story…"Ca-ub, Kiki, ring, ring, ring, run, run, run."

A short time later, another endearing relationship developed when Kiki introduced Caleb to her new client, Gino, who had Down Syndrome and was going deaf and blind. Since Kiki's first time caring for Gino was coming up, she wanted to do a quick drive-by with him so she could meet Gino. Caleb insisted he wanted to stay, so they spent the entire day together. Caleb and Gino shared a touching friendship from the start—one that brought tears to her eyes. They were very attentive to each other's needs. They immediately started holding hands. When Gino's glasses fogged up, Caleb cleared them. When Caleb needed help with his braces, Gino encouraged him to put them on himself. Gino was a very affectionate guy, and kept patting Caleb on his head. Caleb is an extremely tight hugger, but he doesn't usually like to receive affection unless he initiates it. When Gino put his head on Caleb's shoulder, Caleb said, "Are you done yet?"

Gino and Caleb were having such a wonderful time, so Kiki brought them both back to our house. Both Caleb and Gino were obsessed with making photocopies. Gino kept asking Andy, "Can you make a copy of this? Can you make a copy of this one too? Oh, and this one?" Andy graciously kept making copies, and I was thrilled to see that Caleb had found a new friend. Gino was in his forties and owned a home. His caretaker remarked that since they enjoyed each other, she wondered if Caleb wanted to be his roommate. The problem was that Caleb was only 12 years old!

Kiki, Gino, and Caleb witnessed a terrible car accident a few weeks later. Kiki was in the car with two obsessive people. They were traumatized and trying to process what had just happened. Caleb was spiraling out of control and started acting out. Gino firmly planted his feet and shook one finger at him saying, "Caleb, God is looking down on you. Change your attitude."

Caleb and Gino were excited to exchange phone numbers and stay in touch. Caleb's obsessiveness caused him to call Gino often, but Gino usually answered the phone by saying, "Wrong number. Wrong number."

A Shift

There is a time for everything, and a season
for every activity under the heavens.

Ecclesiastes 3:1

I recharged by visiting my parents in Arizona during my spring break. Andy, Jesse, and Kiki watched Caleb so I could spend uninterrupted time with my mom and dad, enjoy the sun and pampering, have heart-to-heart talks with my mom, glean wisdom, and float in the pool. Life was good until it wasn't!

When I came back, Caleb was more irritable and had more meltdowns. He was wrestling to get his way and spiraling out of control. He was wearing shorts when it was snowing. He was just in a fragile place—a time when we knew we had to pick our battles.

Caleb was turning 13, so we began talking about becoming an adult. Kiki began shifting how she worked with him. We wanted to take him to the next level of independence. She told him he didn't need a nanny anymore; instead, she was his life coach. We were trying to help him turn that corner, but Caleb was not quite there. Even though the chronological age was a turning point, Caleb sensed Kiki was pulling away from doing things for him. She was stretching him to do more on his own; our expectations were increasing, and it affected his behavior.

Costco

In preparation for Caleb's 13th birthday party, Kiki offered to take him to Costco. Unfortunately, I didn't foresee my shopping routine with Caleb at Costco as something I should have relayed to Kiki. I should not have had her shop with intention, especially for a birthday party, because it added too much stress for her. I gave Caleb a long leash when we went shopping at Costco. It was a pleasant experience, and I got a lot of shopping done. He would get on the electric cart, and off he went. He wanted to greet others in the electric carts and find out how they got hurt. They often became fast friends, and they would drive around together. Caleb and I would meet up and try all of the samples. I felt that Caleb was relatively safe with the security team at the door since most knew him. Kiki didn't know this, so she was not set up for a successful shopping trip. It was a very different experience for Caleb. Kiki was doing what a nanny should, instructing him to stay with her.

He said, "I want to drive around and get samples."

"Stay with me. We don't have time. We have a list of things to get." With an audience of shoppers, Caleb, who doesn't look like he has a disability when he is in an electric cart, freaked out and pinned her to the meat department cooler with his electric cart. Kiki managed to escape, and then he came up behind her and rammed into her. She went flying.

People were screaming, "What is wrong with you??" They didn't know what had gotten into this crazy person. Hurt, Kiki was on the ground, still defending Caleb, even though he was laughing at her.

"No, no, no…he has special needs. You don't need to call the manager. I'm okay"…even though she was not. Feeling hurt and scared, Kiki ran to her car. Caleb, not feeling an ounce of empathy, chased after her. He charmed his way past the security guard with a cart of groceries, telling him that his nanny was paying for this. He was a madman with stolen merchandise who had just physically assaulted a customer, and he was on a mission to find Kiki in the parking lot. He found her, got out of the cart, and ran through a busy parking lot yelling, "Kiki, Kiki, Kiki!!!" Scared, sobbing, but not engaging him, she called us to rescue her.

Andy managed to help Caleb come back to a sound mind. The reality is this: sometimes this is what having a special needs child looks like. I believe many parents of special needs children can relate. Feeling horrified, Kiki poured out her heart, "I am so afraid he will do this again. I feel like an abused girlfriend. I love him so much, but I can't tell people what is happeneing here, so I'm trying to hide it."

I completely understood.

We felt a heavy burden yet still wanted to share our Caleb connection. We were at a loss about how to move forward. The sad reality was that I could not prepare her for every situation, even with the absolute best care. She didn't know our routine. Caleb was in a bad state of mind. His world went upside down in Costco that day.

As my therapist explained, without even realizing it, Kiki's expectations of staying by her side and her message to become more independent were incongruent. His behavior was frustration-based. He was trying to tell Kiki, "No, this is what we do when we go to Costco." He was expressing what he couldn't verbalize. He had no intention to hurt Kiki, but he didn't understand the impact and consequences of using his electric cart. He could have easily been restrained or pummeled that day by onlookers.

It hurt me in the deepest places of my soul, knowing the public would not understand this. I realized he would have this communication barrier throughout adulthood, and I will not always be at his side. I cannot promise anyone that he won't do this again. He probably won't use an electric cart again because I think he learned from this experience. However, it could, and probably will be something else. He was very remorseful, continuously calling Kiki, "I won't run you over at Costco anymore."

At birth, the neurologist explained that since Caleb has an absent corpus callosum, the area in his brain where empathy is housed will be affected. I have found this fascinating because he can be one of the most compassionate, sympathetic people we know. Yet, other times, we see his lack of empathy. He becomes aggressive and hurtful and doesn't seem to understand its impact on somebody else. It is the reason that he could ram into Kiki with an electric cart and then laugh.

Feeling afraid and defeated, we were back at square one. *What does his future look like? What are we supposed to do?* I didn't need people to tell me the obvious after such a horrific episode. Momma Bear went into overdrive.

After researching online, I made many phone calls, including the University of Wisconsin - Milwaukee and the Clinic for OCD (Obsessive Compulsive Disorder). Of course, he returned my call when I was with my hairdresser. Out of desperation, she cut my hair as I shifted the phone to each ear. Through my tears, I shared, even as the hairdryer was blaring.

This awful ordeal forced me to plan for the future instead of staying stagnant. I learned that I needed to "share the love." I needed more than one person to care for Caleb to prevent burnout and anxiety. The beauty and effectiveness of Kiki is that she values open, honest conversations and always wants what is best for the child.

At times, brain growth may trigger aggressive behavior. Sadly, Caleb could not regulate his emotions that day. This experience taught us that it is good to shift towards autonomy, but it will take time. It will change slowly and may not be by a certain age. He will keep progressing, growing, and learning how to function and adapt to different situations, but it will be over time.

Dr. Tiger

God opened and closed doors until we were led to the right place, Dr. Jeff Tiger and the Tiger Behavior Analysis Research Lab at UWM. Surprisingly, it was even covered by Medicaid! Since it began in 2011, two years prior, Caleb was one of their first clients. Their research aimed to assess and treat his aggressive behaviors of hitting, kicking, scratching, throwing objects at people, pinching, hair pulling, banging into a person either with his body or with another object, and grabbing. Caleb was engaging in problem behavior to receive attention. He needed to develop appropriate communication tools, and we needed to understand how to help him. Dr. Tiger's intervention addressed Caleb's aggressive behavior when he wanted our attention or access to a tangible item. The tools taught were not meant to bring him back from a meltdown but rather to avoid one.

For two months, a team of two ABA (Applied Behavior Analysis) therapists worked with Caleb at our house in his bedroom. They came prepared with wrestling padding in case he became aggressive. One therapist recorded his every move while the other therapist played Xbox with him and deliberately tried to push his buttons to see how he would respond if they took the Xbox away immediately. The goal was to teach Caleb how to use replacement phrases of "Excuse me" and "May I please..." and respond appropriately without being aggressive.

When Caleb said, "Excuse me," and wanted our attention, but we were unable to give it to him, we gave him something tangible to do while he waited for our attention. For example, if I were talking to someone and couldn't be interrupted, I held up one finger and said, "In a minute," and handed him my phone to play with until I was available to talk. We praised him for waiting and provided attention for as long as reasonable.

When Caleb said, "May I please..." and wanted something tangible, but we were unable to give it to him, we gave him our attention while he waited for something tangible. For example, if he wanted to play on my phone, but I didn't want him to have it, I gave him my attention and praised him for his patience.

Their reinforcement phrases were practical, and Caleb made progress with the repetition. The positive reward of attention and something tangible affirmed what I had been doing. Most of the time, I put on a brave face, but below the surface, my mind was trying to stay ahead of Caleb to keep him calm and content. People had no idea that to maintain peace, normalcy, or have a conversation with him forever interrupting me, I constantly did this exchange with him. It is like living with a two-year-old who is just learning to wait his turn. Caleb was older, so people expected him to be able to have better self-control, but he was not there yet. Some felt I was giving in to Caleb, that I didn't teach him manners, or that he was manipulating me. They didn't understand why I would hand my phone to him when he wanted my attention or why I talked to him about a random topic when he wanted something he couldn't have. It was rather affirming to see that it was actually an intervention to avoid meltdowns and aggressive behavior.

What I appreciated most about this program was that Dr. Tiger took the time to meet with various groups of people to explain how to work with him so that we were all on the same page. He met with his teachers, caregivers, and our families to answer questions, discuss the plan, and problem-solve. The consistent approach at school and home helped to curb his meltdowns and aggressive behaviors.

Tim to the Rescue

When Caleb was in high school, Kiki wisely suggested that we look for a male to take him to the next stage in his life. Knowing that Kiki would always be in our family, we agreed. But after having "Kiki extraordinaire" as his  nanny, how would we ever find someone to replace her? That's when God brought Tim into our lives. We met Tim when Caleb participated in the Children's Summer Recreation Program through Balance, an organization whose mission is to support people with disabilities. Tim is extremely patient, fun, calm, and loved by everyone in the special needs community. Caleb doesn't see the need to shower unless he is literally sweating, so he works out with Tim at All Stars Health Center, a gym with personal trainers and classes for individuals with disabilities.

Later, Tim assists Caleb with personal hygiene. The routines have changed over the years, but when COVID-19 hit, their personal hygiene time became virtual. For hours we hear Tim and Caleb playing baseball and bowling on their phones to compare scores, followed by Caleb asking Amazon Alexa to play "Happy Birthday" with every name, language, and dog bark. Caleb laughs heartily as Tim patiently endures his preparation routine to get into the shower. Tim and Caleb have a bond that brings stability and joy to our lives.

SANDY

I shared with my therapist that the most stressful time in my day is getting Caleb ready and out the door at the same time I leave. She stopped me mid-sentence and asked why I was still getting him ready. Even though it was so much faster to help him get ready, I knew it was time to pick this "dressing independently" battle again.

I went home and asked Caleb, "Do you remember Sandy?"

He excitedly exclaimed, "Yes!"

I explained, "Well, she told me I could not get you dressed anymore. Since you are 17 years old now, you need to do this yourself!

Without skipping a beat, he replied, "I don't know Sandy!"

Chapter Resources:

Tiger Center for Applied Behavior Analysis Services
www.tigercenterforaba.com

Balance
www.balanceinc.org

All Stars Health Center
www.allstarhealthcenter.com

The Obsessions Continue

If any of you lacks wisdom, he should ask God, who gives
generously to all without finding fault, and it will be given to him.
James 1:5

According to the National Organization for Disorders of the Corpus Callosum, "Behaviorally individuals with DCC may fall behind their peers in social and problem-solving skills in elementary school or as they approach adolescence... Although a child with DCC may have kept up with his or her peers until this age, as the peer-group begins to make use of an increasingly efficient corpus callosum, the child with DCC falls behind in mental and social functioning. In this way, the behavioral challenges for individuals with DCC may become more evident as they grow into adolescence and young adulthood."

The obsessions continue. Some obsessions are good, and some are messy, complicated, and inappropriate. They are relentless and can make a grown man cry. No amount of discipline will stop them. Even the slightest movement, sound, change of routine, or things out of place exacerbates Caleb's obsessiveness. He is on sensory overload and desperately needs to gain control.

Caleb has been obsessed with hair, nails, massage, and tattoos since about eight years old. He is particularly attracted to girls with long, straight hair, pregnant ladies, and people with tattoos!

As a little boy, Caleb loved brushing his grandma's and babysitter's hair and putting them in ponytails, and it never stopped. He learned a unique braiding style by watching YouTube videos—styling with tight braids, wispy strands, and messy buns. When he was in his early teens, he asked people if he could braid their hair everywhere we went. Many agreed, and some raised an eyebrow.

Caleb also loved to paint family and friends' fingernails and toenails. His nail polishing precision was lacking, but it brought joy, conversation, and beauty.

Another obsession was massage. Caleb always asked people, "Are you stressed? Are you tight? Do you want me to help you? It will make you feel better. Can I give you a massage?" Caleb has strong hands and stamina that can outlast everyone. People lined up for his hand and back massages because he was that good, while others squirmed with uneasiness.

Last but not least, tattoos. He is obsessed with tattoo designs. He always wants to know if they hurt and if he can have one. He is mesmerized by watching videos of tattoo artists creating artistry. Whenever he sees someone with a tattoo, he usually strikes up a conversation about their tattoo.

Caleb receives many mixed messages regarding these obsessions. Many people rave and thank him profusely, while others are uneasy and speak volumes with their body language. Unfortunately, he doesn't read social cues, so it is confusing to him. People feel uncomfortable when a young man asks if they want their hair braided or need a massage. I get it...*Trust me! The problem is helping him to understand.* We have an unbelievable amount of conversations with Caleb regarding personal space, what is appropriate, and what is not.

Why the obsession with hair, nails, massage, and tattoos? We have many theories, but we will never know. Perhaps it's his creative, artsy side? Does he want to connect with ladies? He likes deep sensory input. Does he want to help people feel better? All of the above?

When he was a young teen and could see that the obsession was not going away, we began to think of ways to make it healthy and positive. We fed into his desire to create beauty because we could see how much joy it brought to others and him. He spent hours organizing his lotions and fingernail polishes and cutting tattoos at home.

Caleb was often asked to provide an entertainment table with tattoos at parties. Kids eagerly waited for him to create tattoos on their faces, arms, and legs, and colorful ribbons with their new dos. We loved to see him content and feel purposeful. It also allowed us to mingle at parties without disengaging from conversations to respond to him.

Prior to having a creative outlet at parties, Caleb was always by our side, constantly interrupting our discussions. Teaching him was exhausting, yet I always smiled so I didn't create a scene. As much as Andy and I needed to socialize and be with people, it was hard to keep him entertained. He didn't run off and play with the kids because he didn't fit in. He could relate to adults and wanted to be a part of our conversations. Having him interrupt and interject in all of our conversations was hard. I'm sure it bothered others as well.

Once, my sisters tried their best to get him to play with the kids. They felt terrible because they could see that it turned Caleb inside out and upside down obsessive. It wasn't worth it. Looking back, I think it was a

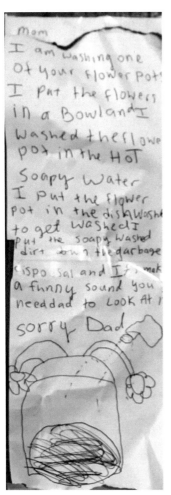

blessing in disguise that Caleb sat with the adults for many years. He was extremely observant, so he learned to converse and picked up my storytelling mannerisms. But as a young teen, he had an outlet at parties to be creative as a manicurist, hairdresser, and paper tattoo artist.

Whether heartwarming or cringeworthy, Caleb's obsessive world becomes ours, and we work tirelessly to work it through with him.

Worth a Giggle

Caleb's obsessiveness is quirky. When he was a teenager, he was obsessed with cleaning everything. He cleaned the dust out of pill bottles, the wax out of candle jars, and the dirt out of plants. One day we came home to this gem:

Mom
I am washing one of your flower pots. I put the flowers in a Bowl and I washed the flower pot in the Hot soapy water. I put the flower pot in the dishwasher to get washed. I put the soapy washed dirt down the garbage disposal, and Its making a funny sound. You need to Look At it. sorry Dad

SALLY

Beginning in middle school, Caleb went shopping at Sendik's with a grocery list by himself. I followed up by checking the cart and paying with a credit card. It works for us. At times it was total role reversal as I sat in the car collecting my thoughts while he shopped. One day, while sitting in the parking lot at Sendik's, I saw our sweet neighbor and friend, Sally. God put her in my path at just the right moment. Through the tears, I shared

that Andy and I needed to get away to process some devastating news.

Our idea was camping. She called the next day to say she prayed for us and wanted to help. She arranged for us to stay at a bed and breakfast near Door County for two nights!

Sally is our godly encourager. She loves our family and has a special bond with Caleb. Caleb and I have many laughs and tender moments with her, but most of all, we know we have a prayer partner in Sally.

DWIGHT

Our beloved school bus driver, Dwight, is a patient man who makes everyone feel special. One memory in particular still brings me joy. Caleb had a hard time catching the bus on time. One day he was eager to show his friends the dog, Chewie, we were dogsitting. When Caleb saw the bus coming, he scooted out with Chewie as fast as possible. Caleb's friend, Breanna shouted, "Caleb's ready. Let's dance!" Everyone on the bus did a little jig. Breanna shook her entire body as she danced in her wheelchair, waving her arms. Katie and Cassie clapped their hands, making large hand gestures. Breanna yelled, "Chad, stand up and shake your booty!" So he did. Robert lifted one leg up and down as high as possible, causing his feeding tube to loosen.

I asked Caleb, "What did you do then?"

He said, "We cleaned up the mess and kept dancing."

Turning a Corner

Caleb had a calm, compassionate middle school teacher. As it turned out, his teacher and I went to high school together. He was willing to lean on me for suggestions on how to work with Caleb. One day, Caleb was not cooperating. He was stuck, and nothing was working. His teacher called me to see what I thought might work. To his surprise, I asked if they had any laundry that needed folding. Since it was a living skills classroom, they had plenty of dishtowels. Having Caleb fold laundry snapped him out of the obsessive, frozen state and helped him turn a corner. At that moment, it was not about having him "obey because I said so." It was about how to get him to turn the corner, flip his brain, and restore order in his brain so that he could move past it. Caleb's day immediately turned around, and his teacher was thankful for another strategy.

For Caleb's eigth grade graduation, Andy and I told the teacher that it would mean a lot to us if he could walk down the aisle rather than use his wheelchair. As the classmates filed in, Caleb greeted people as he walked down the aisle. After he received his diploma, he walked back down the aisle, gave me a big hug, and handed his diploma to me…an endearing moment.

WHIPPED CREAM GUZZLE

It was the morning after Thanksgiving, and Caleb was obsessed with spraying the entire can of whipped cream into his mouth. We often hid things in the refrigerator, the garage, or the basement, but here he was again, guzzling whipped cream. I always threatened to feed it to the squirrels, but this time I wrestled it from him and chucked it out into our backyard woods. He was upset that I threw it out there, but then he yelled, "You forgot the cap!" Even in his fit, he needed closure, knowing the cap belonged on the can, so I chucked the cap out in the woods too. Since he couldn't calm down, my plan backfired. I had to go outside, find the can and the cap in the woods, and bring them back inside so he could calm down. At times, it is necessary to go back on your word.

God's Healing Hand

So do not fear, for I am with you; do not be dismayed,
for I am your God. I will strengthen you and help you;
I will uphold you with My righteous right hand.

Isaiah 41:10

Surgeries

By the grace of God, Caleb has been able to avoid having continuous surgeries in his life. As a child, he had serial casting and botox injections in his hamstrings and heel cords to help him flex better, but we are constantly in awe that Caleb does not complain about pain. Looking at him, and especially his X-rays, it is a wonder how he moves with his hips and spine out of alignment, his heel cords, hamstrings, feet, and ankles tight as can be, and his toes deformed and tucked beneath his feet. God graciously gave Caleb a high pain tolerance, or maybe he doesn't have feeling, but it is God's gift to alleviate chronic pain.

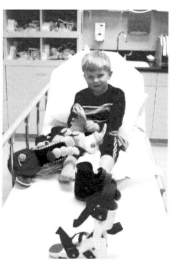

The most challenging and demanding time was when the orthopedic surgeon explained following a gait study that Caleb had

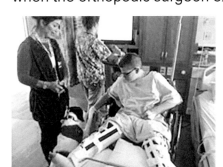

to have three surgeries back-to-back, one requiring complete casting with a bar placed between both legs. The thought of this was extremely overwhelming. *How are we going to keep him still for all of these months? How will we lift him? Care for him? Keep him content?* But again, God was faithful to provide. In preparation, we arranged for in-home therapists, caretakers, and a social calendar for visitors. Friends and family stepped in to hold us up when we were weak. Rather than a Christmas tree that year, we had a hospital bed and commode in our living room.

In order to get Caleb to cooperate with painful procedures, he would often make a deal with nurses. They would allow him to braid their hair after he received his shot. If there was a therapy dog available, Caleb was beyond excited. One time, he insisted that a particular nurse hold his hand while the podiatrist did a procedure. Embarrassed, yet knowing he would cooperate if this happened, I made the necessary request to the podiatrist. He obliged and asked the nurse passing by to help him out. Dejected yet smiling, she came out of the room minutes later. "Wrong nurse. Caleb wants Melissa."

Never Without

Money was tight, but we were never without. We often lived paycheck to paycheck, which added to our stress. However, we were always amazed at how God took care of us. I grew up loving to go to rummage sales with my mom, so I have that "rummage sale adrenaline rush" in my blood. Time after time, I would find the most specific needs and desires at rummage sales. Oftentimes we could not see how we could possibly pay for the looming expense. The Lord was always faithful to provide whether we received an unexpected check, a rebate, a tax return, food pantry items, or the Lord laying it on someone's heart to give us an anonymous gift. The more He cared for us, the easier it was to trust Him with our finances. Looking back, it was a season of learning to humbly receive money and services at a time when we could not bring in any more income. When our financial situation changed, it allowed us to pay it forward. We are always grateful for God's provision.

GENEROSITY OF A STRANGER

We had just switched health insurance companies, and we were down to our last $40. When I went to pay for three prescriptions, it came to $300. I didn't have $300, so I needed other options. A man with a lisp who overheard my conversation with the pharmacist asked, "How much more do you need?" Sadly, I couldn't understand him, so he repeated it three times. I teared up when I realized that he was offering to pay for the remaining cost of one of the drugs so that I could at least buy one. His kindness and generosity of $10 powerfully impacted me. I assured him the Lord would bless him abundantly for his willingness to help a stranger. Again and again, the Lord provided daily.

Memory Moment

I always love to make memories. It usually doesn't cost much, but it takes extra effort. When Caleb was 16 years old, a church about an hour away had "A Night to Shine." It was similar to Tim Tebow's mission, with a prom-like atmosphere for people with special needs. I was so impressed with this extraordinary night! Before that evening, Men's Wearhouse fit them for a complimentary tuxedo rental. Upon arrival, hairdressers were available for primping and updos. Limousines drove them to the church, where they were met with a red carpet experience. Everyone was escorted to the prom by their date. The audience cheered and held signs as the emcee called their names, and they entered the church under the American flag hoisted by a fire engine. Once inside, they had dinner, danced, and conducted photo shoots while parents embraced the moment through video nearby. They truly had a Night to Shine.

Blessings Flow

*Every good and perfect gift is from above, coming down from the Father
of the heavenly lights, who does not change like shifting shadows.*

James 1:17

Xander

After meeting Danielle's dog, Sadie, we knew we needed to get a dog for Caleb and Jesse. We had Augie, a rescue dog, for a few short months, but unfortunately, Augie never bonded with us. Sadly, he ran away from home and was hit by a car.

We were reluctant to adopt another rescue dog, but in 2016, God sent us an angel in Xander. We decided to give Tailwaggers 911 a try since they let the dog stay at your house for a few days to see if it is a good fit. As only God could, Xander arrived through special delivery and answered prayer.

Xander was a two-year-old rescue dog. He was found with another dog in the fields of Georgia. Tailwaggers 911 Dog Rescue brought him to Wisconsin. When the foster family brought Xander to our house, we immediately knew he was a good fit. Since Caleb is not always steady on his feet, we needed a dog that was not hyper. Xander is about as mellow as a dog can be. His

Xander

original name was Zeus. We changed it to Zander and then decided that he had the X-factor, so we changed it to Xander with an "X." Because of his stunning copper-colored eyes, his full name is Xander Copper Griswold.

Xander's calm personality is highly unusual but precisely what we needed. He rarely barks and doesn't jump, lick, or drool. He is rather stoic and regal. Most importantly, he is acutely tuned in to Caleb. With every move Caleb makes, Xander attentively watches and desires his love and attention. Xander waits in the driveway for Caleb to return. When my sister watched him for a long weekend, she couldn't believe it. Xander did not eat, pee, or poop for days. He was depressed and hid in the bushes until Caleb returned.

Variety Bike

Caleb loved to ride his motorized vehicles, but he eventually couldn't squeeze himself in and out of it anymore. I saw a blurb in Variety—the Children's Charity of Wisconsin newsletter for an opportunity to receive a bike. Variety's mission is "dedicated to enriching the lives of children with physical or developmental needs and their families." We could enter our story, and those chosen would receive an adaptive tricycle through a grant. Since Caleb's therapist had tried him on bikes before, we knew he would love them, but they cost thousands of dollars! Here was our chance, and worth a try. I took advantage of these opportunities as I felt led. This was the beginning of something extraordinary!

As only God could make this happen, Caleb was awarded an adaptive bike! On the day of the awarding, families were at the theater parking lot, where a track was set up to have siblings and recipients ride the bikes. I thought getting Jesse involved in the fun was brilliant because it's usually hard for the siblings when the special needs child receives all of the attention. Caleb had his own wheels, and he was in heaven!

After several years, he outgrew his adaptive tricycle. Variety stated they would exchange it for a larger bike when needed. Again I had to complete the application to upgrade, and he was chosen as the recipient of a recumbent bike. The presentation occurred at the Grand Geneva in Lake Geneva, Wisconsin, before a roomful of business donors. Caleb's name was announced, and we both went forward. I gave his acceptance speech—not realizing that he was eagerly waiting behind me to talk to the audience. This was the day, when he was 16 years old, I realized that Caleb loved public speaking! He was completely himself, connecting with his audience, telling them about Muttland Meadows and how much dog poop he loved to pick up at the dog park.

When Caleb and I went to Variety to finalize details for his new bike, the director invited us to her lake house for a day of fun in the sun! I thought, *Wow! Yes, that would be awesome! We don't usually get invited to the lake with people who understand our crazy life! Jesse would have a blast!* Andy had to work, but a day on the lake was just what I needed. She gave me the directions, we put them in our GPS, and off we went the next day. It was a spur-of-the-moment decision, and we would "make a memory." My expectation of a relaxing day quickly turned stressful on the road. The lake was much further away than I realized! We were in the boonies and lost our internet connection. I had no idea where we were going, and Caleb had a meltdown. Again, my right-hand man, Jesse, was frantically trying everything to get directions as we went in and out of internet service. Finally, stressed and lost, he asked, "Who are these people anyway?" I tried to explain, but his response made me realize that not everyone is as crazy as I am...

"You mean to tell me we don't even know these people?!"

We finally made it to the lake and ended up having a blast, creating another memory that day!

Caleb used his bike for absolutely everything and every season. In the summer, he visited neighbors, watched them work, and chatted as he went around the block. He tied a wagon to the back of his bike and hauled everything imaginable. In the fall, he secured a dog leash to the back of his bike, dragging the rake behind him. In winter, it was a shovel. He was innovative and determined to maximize his bike. An endearing scene was watching Caleb load Xander onto his bike to give him a ride across the invisible line because Xander thought he would get zapped with his collar.

I loved having the break when he rode his bike around the block. Just because we gave him more independence did not mean he had free reign to go wherever he wanted, or we weren't holding him accountable. We kept tabs on him by giving him our phone with Find My Phone in his pocket or waited patiently and expectantly for his return around the corner. However, one day I fell asleep in those twenty minutes of waiting, and we got a phone call from a dog walker that Caleb was hanging out at their house and playing cards with another special needs girl around the block. I'm thankful for God's protection and assurance earlier on in his life that He would take better care of him than I ever could.

Chapter Resource:

Variety - the Children's Charity of Wisconsin
www.varietywi.org

A Servant's Heart

Let Your face shine on Your servant; save me in Your unfailing love.

Psalm 31:16

Mayor of Muttland Meadows

When Caleb was 16 years old, he loved to go to Muttland Meadows by himself. It didn't take long for him to build relationships with friends. They loved on him as he loved on their dogs, and I knew this community was looking out for Caleb and Xander. Thus began Caleb's dog ministry at Muttland Meadows. Every night he filled gallons upon gallons of empty milk jugs with water. He filled 20+ gallons of water on a typical night, but eventually, that number grew. He loaded them in our truck, and when we dropped him off the next day, he dutifully loaded them in his wagon. Caleb began his morning by greeting the dogs and owners by name. At times, the dog park is a picture of heaven with people of diverse

backgrounds walking the same trails with a shared love—dogs playing in the green grass on a sunny day.

With his awkward gait, Caleb began his daily route pulling his wagon with Xander in work mode, attentively keeping pace. They stopped at each water dish to fill it with fresh water. As they came to a mailbox along the way, they stopped to ensure enough plastic poop bags were stocked. He shuffled merrily along the woodchip paths throwing sticks to frolicking dogs and conversing with everyone he passed. Eventually, he came equipped with a toolbelt containing sunscreen, bug spray, a dog leash, treats, tennis balls, and poop bags.

After making his rounds, he sat on the bench at the front gate, waiting for his dog-walking crew to arrive at 10 a.m. every morning. Eager to help, Caleb met Kasey at her car to help get George, Cuddles, Chewie, Charlie,

and company into the gate. Caleb and his dog-walker friends exercised daily on the trails, but it was much more than a dog walk. They shared incredible bonding and love. When Marlene's dog, Sugar, was sick, he prayed for her. Xander guided the blind dog, Tenney, when she was going off the path, and Tenney learned to follow Caleb's voice. When dogs died, he wrote out sympathy cards. I knew Caleb had a whole world of dog friends when I pulled up to a stoplight with the car window down one day. Caleb said, "Hi Otis!" to the dog next to him.

People often commented to me how welcoming and kind-hearted Caleb was to them. His memory for names, both dogs and people, is unbelievable. It makes people feel welcomed, loved, and special. He loved helping owners get their energetic dogs uphill to the front gate and into their cars. Caleb loved to do one of the most disgusting jobs, picking up dog poop. It was a great day when he could pick up 50+ poops.

To see Caleb's ownership of the park unfold as he welcomed dogs and their owners were touching and heartwarming. He was in his happy place with no one rushing him around, no expectations, just loving dogs and keeping the dog park running smoothly.

He affectionately became known as the Mayor of Muttland Meadows.

Caleb loved to stay at the dog park all day. He did not want to come home. Early on, a concerned dog owner called the police, who told us this person was worried because Caleb was always there. *Who were his parents? Did they not want him at home? Did Caleb have enough food and water?* "He has 20+ gallons of water, to be exact."

One day as I was dropping Caleb off, he instructed me, "Don't come to pick me up until it is dark out. Don't come when the sky is blue. Don't come when the sky is pink. Come when the sky is black."

One day a dog park walker messaged me to say that his dog passed away, so he needed to take his other dog, Maggie, to Muttland Meadows to socialize. He was only there for about 20 minutes but immediately connected with Caleb. The next day Caleb greeted Maggie and him by name. He said, "The work he puts into that park physically isn't anything compared to the love he spreads through those acres. You raised an incredible young man and needed to let you know." I was touched and posted it on Facebook. I told Caleb this quote was from a stranger. He corrected me, "He's not a stranger." In his mind, there are no strangers. They are all just friends. Another dog lover noted that many volunteers spread woodchips on Spring Clean Up Day. It was sweltering hot, and so many people were taking a break. Not Caleb. He struggled to push a wheelbarrow of woodchips up the hill. Watching him work so hard motivated them to get moving. She later realized why it was tough to push the wheelbarrow; the wheel was flat!

Caleb is very observant. He could tell who was at the park as we drove by just by looking at the cars in the parking lot. He is also innovative. To carry many empty milk jugs, he strung them on a dog leash and looped them around his waist.

Caleb continued to expand his job description, and even though it often meant more effort, we loved his initiative and desire to meet the need. Since the poop bags needed replenishing, he called the managers at Pick 'n Save and Meier and explained that he would like to use their recycled plastic bags for the dog park. He also brought our weedwhacker and cut down the weeds in the park. One of the nasty jobs he did periodically was to bring home all the gross dog dishes and wash them in our dishwasher…yuck! Again, as often as we tried to say "no," he wouldn't let it go. I knew it was another obsession because one snowy evening, he insisted that we go to the dog park to pick up the water dishes so he could wash them. My heart filled with compassion as I sat in my car, watching him trek through the snow, looking for the dishes under the snow. It has to be challenging to be him sometimes. He returned to the car and said, "It was hard to find them!"

The Muttland Meadows dog park walkers appreciated Caleb's generous,

giving heart, so they honored him with a plaque on the bench where he and Xander sat all the time. It says "Caleb's Corner." We will always be grateful for how Muttland Meadows dogs and dog walkers embraced Caleb and Xander with open arms and hearts.

Extraordinary Citizen Award

In 2016, Caleb was honored to receive the "Extraordinary Citizen" award from

Partnership Bank in Cedarburg. Seeing our village of family, friends, and Muttland Meadows dog lovers gather together to see Caleb receive this award was beautiful. I shared our testimony as Caleb was chomping at the bit to speak at the microphone. Once again, he was completely comfortable interacting and engaging with his audience.

Caleb's World

Caleb tended to the dog park because he loved it. He wasn't doing it for attention or accolades, but that is what he received. Many pups and people felt Caleb's heart.

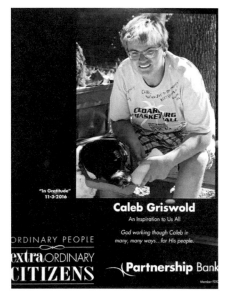

"In Gratitude" 11-3-2016

ORDINARY PEOPLE

extra ORDINARY

CITIZENS

Caleb Griswold

An Inspiration to Us All

God working though Caleb in many, many ways...for His people.

Partnership Bank

Member FDIC

News Graphic and Ozaukee Press wrote articles, and Fox News filmed "Caleb's World." Caleb was oblivious to the attention of journalists and photographers. He thought all of it was normal. Caleb's miraculous story was being told; we were thrilled and honored.

Guideposts Magazine

My mom's lifelong dream was to have one of her articles published in Guideposts. To our amazement, her dream came true when Guideposts, which reaches 2 million people worldwide, accepted her story for the March 2018 issue. With our input, an editor from Guideposts rewrote and revised the article.

After the article was published, we were amazed at the outpouring of love from strangers from across the United States who took the time to encourage and reach out to us. We received published dog books from a fellow dog -lover author, crocheted gifts and bookmarks with words of encouragement, and even a young mother in Norway whose son was recently diagnosed with a similar brain disorder connected with us. She appreciated Caleb's story of hope and encouragement for their journey. Locally, as the Mayor of Muttland Meadows, he was invited to do a Meet and Greet at a Paws for a Cause event in Cedarburg.

But the most surprising phone call came from the Grafton Police Chief while I was teaching. All I could think was, *Oh, no! Who's in trouble? Caleb or Jesse?*

Instead, he said, "Apparently, your son is the Mayor of Muttland Meadows." Linda, from Virginia, read the article in *Guideposts*. She was so touched by it that she wrote a heartwarming letter to Caleb. Her late daughter Lisa loved animals and wanted to be a vet. Sadly she died from brain cancer, so she wanted to give Caleb a check in her honor. Wanting to make sure that he received it, she explained to the police department in a letter that the envelope was open because, in this crazy world, she didn't want them to think there was anything illegal in the mail. The police chief was choked up to see such a beautiful gesture. His secretary exclaimed, "I know Caleb. He volunteers at the Ozaukee Humane Society, and he is extraordinary."

He proudly handed it to me at the police station and explained that he had to open the envelope in a particular room because he wasn't sure if an explosive was inside. To his surprise, it was an explosive letter of love. Linda later sent thoughtful gifts, including the matching Mayor of Muttland Meadows hats for Caleb and Xander.

Humane Society

Caleb volunteers at the Ozaukee Humane Society in the Shelter Crew. He loads the washer and dryer, folds the towels, adds peanut butter to the toy Kongs, cuts hot dogs, shreds newspaper for the bunnies, organizes, and, with Andy's help, takes unneeded donations to Goodwill. He loves it and takes his job very seriously.

While folding the laundry, he noticed the blankets had frayed edges. He didn't want the cats to choke, so he brought them home and cut off the loose threads. When he learned to sew, he brought home the blankets with holes and sewed them into smaller blankets for the cats.

As with most of his volunteer jobs, it is hard to get him to leave. Understandably, the coordinators often call to say that his volunteering is appreciated, but others also want to contribute. I let him work it out by himself whenever possible. This email exchange touched my heart to hear Caleb

explain his reason, and Ashley respectfully worked it through with him to solve the problem.

Hi Ashley!

It's Caleb Griswold; why aren't you letting me stay at the WHS. I am letting "Susie" do her 12-2:30 shift I Am shredding paper for the rabbits during her time then I am doing the rest from 2 until 6 I don't want the laundry to get moldy and gross 😿 that's why I stay long it's because my Grandma Johnson passed away in September 2020 and I miss her and I have nothing to do at home that's why I like staying at the WHS if she didn't die I would not of stayed that long see you Saturday

Caleb

Hi Caleb!

Thanks for reaching out and sorry for the delay. It has been a busy week! I am sorry to hear about your Grandma Johnson. Losing a loved one is never easy! 😢

How about I stop in one Saturday this month and we can chat about your volunteering time and maybe some other tasks you can do besides shredding paper during other volunteer shifts!

We appreciate all the hard work you put in to make sure the laundry is clean and free of mold!!

Thanks!

Ashley

Chuckle For The Day

While Caleb was training to be a volunteer at the Ozaukee Humane Society, he insisted that I wear my humane society t-shirt. I quickly washed it but didn't have time to dry it. 'Don't mind me; I am happy to wear my cold, wet shirt.' Sometimes we chuckle at what we do to keep him moving in the right direction, sometimes we cry, and sometimes, all we can say is, "Wow, just wow."

Canine Good Citizen

Since Xander has a docile temperament, Caleb trained Xander to be a Canine Good Citizen. With Caleb as his master, Xander had to pass a 10-step test which included greeting, slamming a phone book behind him without any flinching, and Caleb leaving his sight without reacting. Caleb and

Xander passed the test the first time to our wonderful surprise. With this certificate, Caleb and Xander could go into nursing homes, schools, and stores.

Xander, the Comfort Dog

Comfort Dogs are wonderful additions to a school. When my administrator commented that she was looking for a trained dog, I knew Xander was up for the job. Caleb and I were invited to introduce Xander at an assembly as the Comfort Dog for USM. Xander loves to go to school with me three times a week. He stays near me in the Academic Resource Center doing his one and only trick—lying in the hallway as students, administrators, and staff pet him all day long. Xander is in the yearbook, right next to the administrators.

Noticing the Elderly

Caleb loves to take Xander to the nursing home to visit his friends. It began when he visited a new friend, Vi, from our church. He didn't take long to develop many friendships with the residents and families. Sadly, when Caleb first arrived, he checked the board to see which of his friends had died and joined his other friends in heaven.

Caleb and Xander walked from wing to wing and floor to floor, knocking on people's doors to see if they wanted visitors. Xander and Caleb had regulars that looked forward to their visits. The slow pace of activity is the pace that Caleb thrives. No hurry to get anywhere—just taking life as it comes. Not only did he have fun bonding with the residents, but he also became equally attached to their loved ones who sat with them all day. I knew I would want a Caleb and Xander visit if my parents were at a nursing home.

Residents often gave him candy and stuffed animals from BINGO to show appreciation. He walked them to the dining room, put on their bibs, and sat with them as they ate dinner.

After many visits, Caleb invited my mom, Grandma Just, to meet Vi and see his unfolding nursing home ministry. Before they left, my mom asked Vi if she could pray for her. "Absolutely!" Vi expressed her gratitude. That small act made an indelible impression on Caleb. From that day forward, he wanted to pray for people.

On Sunday afternoons, he loved to wheel friends to the chapel. He helped in the services by putting blankets on their laps, finding the right songbook pages, and tending to their needs. As he shared his devotion as a substitute chaplain one day, I could see this was all preparation for whatever God had in store for his future. Love and compassion oozed from Caleb as he propped up a grandpa leaning in his wheelchair. He sat still the whole service so the grandpa would sit up straight. Following the chapel service, he gathered several residents into a room to read the Bible to them. Someone commented that Caleb needed a larger print. He began typing the Bible verses, enlarging and printing them, and putting them into plastic sleeves and binders for everyone. He gathered several friends into a room for what he called his "sermon after the sermon."

He also gathered and read *Little Visits With God,* a devotional my mom used to read to us. When I was little, my mom started a nursing home ministry where my grandma and grandpa lived. It began with *Little Visits With God* in my grandma's room and grew to services in the large dining room. Unbeknownst to Caleb, I loved wheeling people to the chapel, passing out songbooks, and helping them find page numbers. To see Caleb have grandma's heart is heartwarming.

As he spent more and more time there, the maintenance crew showed Caleb the secret passage in the basement. He was beyond excited to find the beauty shop! He stopped and asked the hairdresser if she needed help, and she did! She later told me that he was such a godsend that day. She

didn't know how she could do everything she needed to do that day, and Caleb appeared and asked if she needed help. He wheeled residents to and from their appointments, swept hair, did laundry, and even got to take rollers out of a grandma's hair. The volunteer coordinator later called to ask for Caleb's availability because the hairdresser wanted him to work in the salon. Since the high school was looking for community connections, I advocated for Caleb to spend one school day afternoon at the nursing home's hair salon during his sophomore year. It was a learning experience that stretched him, used his gifts, and built independence.

Because Caleb has an obsessive personality, he began spending much of his free time at the nursing home. It was very hard for me to get him to leave. The director received complaints from some nurses that Caleb was overstaying his welcome. He also made some nurses uncomfortable because he was intrigued by those who had tattoos and wanted to pray with others. I understood the need for the nursing staff to set boundaries, and I used it as a teaching opportunity for him, but it was difficult for him to understand. We wanted him to continue to see his friends, but I didn't have the time or energy to stay with him as a volunteer.

We still run into relatives of those living in the community. They express their thanks to Caleb for visiting their loved ones; others beg him to go back. The love shared was mutual!

Joie de Vivre

He especially loved his endearing friend, Dottie, a godly, sharp 90-year-old grandma. They shared many laughs together at the nursing home. She especially liked when Caleb braided her hair because he braided it as tightly as she liked it.

Since we had the privilege of going to church together, one Sunday, we shared a heart-to-heart moment. "This could not have been easy. How is it that you have kept your joy?"

"I would say it is because God brings key people into our lives to help with what we are going through at that time," I responded.

She then asked, "This had to have been hard on Jesse. How did that go?"

I explained how they complement each other. Jesse hit the milestones and helped Caleb meet them as a child. In middle school, they had separate lives because there was no need to burden Jesse with Caleb's needs. Now, as young adults, they are coming back together. We cannot underestimate how difficult this has been on Jesse; however, it has developed qualities in him that could only come from living with a brother with special needs—qualities of patience, problem-solving skills, and adaptability.

When I told her I was writing a book, she said I should title it *Joie de Vivre - Exuberant Enjoyment of Life*. That is Caleb. A few years later, when Dottie was in hospice, her daughter Jennifer texted Caleb to say that she braided Dottie's hair one last time so that it was braided nicely for when she saw Jesus. Caleb had the honor of speaking at Dottie's funeral. Jennifer said the memory that always made her smile was the day he excitedly hugged Dottie at church, and they tipped into the pew and giggled. He shared that story at her funeral, and I told Jennifer that listeners were probably horrified. She assured me they always chuckled when they reminisced about that embrace with impact.

"Treat Every Day Like Christmas!" -Elf

Caleb reminds me of a cross between Forrest Gump and Elf. This picture captures his childlike, fun-loving outlook on life. 'It's Christmas. Why wouldn't I wear my Santa outfit to the movies?' Oh, to live life without embarrassment or self-consciousness.

Chapter Resources:

Fox News
www.fox6now.com/news/hes-perfect-in-his-own-way-cedarburg-teen-with-rare-brain-disorder-thrives-as-a-volunteer

 Scan here to watch!

Muttland Meadows
www.muttlandmeadows.org

Canine Good Citizen
www.akc.org/products-services/training-programs/canine-good-citizen

For the *News Graphic* article, scan here:

For the *Ozaukee Press* article, scan here:

For the *Guidposts* article, scan here:

Block and Delete

Let us approach the throne of grace with confidence, so that we may receive mercy and find grace to help us in our time of need.

Hebrews 4:16

Social media is a blessing and a curse, especially for many with special needs. Caleb has a strong social gene, so Facebook allows him to engage and connect with others. However, his chronological age doesn't match his cognitive age. He has the body of a man with hormones but the obsessive mind of a five-year-old.

Caleb has an innate ability to navigate the computer, partly because he has no fear. We love the computer for him because it is his lifeline in many respects. We want him to keep up with the times electronically, or else he will not have a way to communicate and express himself. It will isolate him from society if he doesn't maintain his computer skills. Our belief has always been to teach him how to use it appropriately. He has devised a keyboarding style that works for him and loves to type lists, letters, and sermon notes on his computer. He also excels in Photoshop and Illustrator.

Xander Christmas

One of the first apps he discovered was Words with Friends, an online Scrabble game to play with Facebook friends and strangers. It occupied his time to play before bed. It gave us a break from entertaining him. It was a harmless, benign word game. *What could be bad about that?* He discovered he could chat with people, friends, and strangers. At first, they were friendly discussions, but then he began to ask my friends and strangers personal questions.

The conversation was an obsessive and repetitive loop. Caleb's end of the conversation often went like this:

Do you have a tattoo?

Where is your tattoo?

Did it hurt?

Are you stressed?

Do you need prayer?

Would you like me to give you a massage to calm you down?

Yes or no??

Hard or soft??

???

Answer me.

As you can imagine, the responses were varied. Most said that they just wanted to play the game. Caleb was usually okay with that because he would go on to the next person. For him, it was like fishing; if someone responded, he was excited he caught one. Some stopped playing Words with Friends with him. Some politely answered and tried to redirect him. Others thought he was a pervert, swore, and were very upset.

Since we both have Apple phones, we have Family Sharing, which allows us to set parental controls. I block and delete people I do not want him talking to, edit inappropriate comments on Facebook, and continuously monitor his activity.

After a while, he moved to Facebook Messenger. Again, he was having conversations with my friends and strangers. He joined tattoo groups and communicated with them on Messenger. Some are from other countries, so they communicate with symbols and a translator. Trying and block and delete Caleb's obsessive conversations has been maddening.

Caleb: I'm interested.

Tattoo artist: Great. I can give you a tattoo.

Caleb: I do tattoos too.

Tattoo artist: Awesome. What kind?

Caleb: Paper.

Other times he joined massage groups.

Are you stressed?

Do you want me to give you a massage?

Hard or soft?

Yes or no?

It was the same loop he would say to everyone, but the responses were usually disgusting. We explained to him in many ways that people with disgusting responses are "creepy people," and you are being creepy. Whenever we ask him, "Why?? Why do you talk to these creepy people?" With quivering lips, often while banging his head on the floor, he either answers, "They talk to me," or, "They want me to help calm them down."

In desperation, we begged every Geek Squad member, Apple Store expert, and computer-savvy friend for advice. Even though we have parental control over his screen time, it requires excessive monitoring. Part of the issue is that he is not a child. He is a young man who wants to connect with people and is learning appropriate computer usage and boundaries.

It is easy to listen to the voices in my head or the voices of others.

You are a terrible parent.

All you need to do is…I would never allow my child…

You should never have allowed him to start on the computer.

The evil one is coming for him.

Shame on you! Of course, you need to monitor him; it is your child.

We keep Caleb busy with daily routine activities, probably more than most would believe or commit to doing. He is not on electronics all day. We sometimes wish he would watch TV or a movie; it doesn't hold his interest. His mind is always going, and he wants to be doing something.

Our phones are also necessary. When needed, he has a Gabb phone, which is a phone that doesn't have access to the internet, social media, or games. However, there are many times and many reasons that I allow him to use my phone. I may hand him my phone to entertain him so I can have a conversation with someone without any interruptions, have quiet time, allow him to connect with his friends and family, and call Shared Ride Taxi…The list is endless. We need the flexibility of phone and computer usage. The reality is that we are not going to take it away entirely. We rely on it all the time.

We continue to seek God for wisdom regarding this issue. What would God have us do for Caleb in this situation? Not what others "know" they would do if they were in this situation. Our priority is to protect him as he goes through different stages of his life.

STRANGERS

We stopped at Culver's since I was anxious to hear about his time at Wisconsin Lions Camp in Rosholt, Wisconsin. He planted his feet and shook his booty as we stood in line. As a stranger commented on his dance, he exclaimed, "We will beat you getting our food. Can we sit with you?" As I brought my food into the dining room, Caleb and Marilyn, the stranger we had just met two minutes ago, were smiling and enjoying each other's company. We shared a beautiful connection about the Lord, dogs, and our sons. I love when the Lord weaves sweet, encouraging encounters into our days. She later posted a picture on Facebook and commented, "I met Jesus today in these two people." Caleb read the post and said, "I'm not Jesus!"

Chapter Resource:

Wisconsin Lions Camp
www.wisconsinlionscamp.com

A Burst of Creativity

For we are all God's handiwork, created in Christ Jesus to
do good works, which God prepared in advance for us to do.

Ephesians 2:10

When Caleb was little, all his friends and classmates were off, running around outside and having a great time. Since he couldn't walk, I spent a lot of time with him creating and being artistic because it was something we both loved. When the boys were nine and ten years old, they both participated in the Plein Air Festival in downtown Cedarburg. Little did I know that all that time, exposure, and skills development prepared him for a future in art.

Caleb's world opened up when he got to high school. He loved attending school to see all his friends, students, teachers, secretaries, cooks, administrators, janitors…everyone. He had a "good morning" route, greeting the district office ladies and the principal. Of course, he loved the candy they gave him, but it was also built-in social skills training.

Early on in high school, Caleb's art teacher, Deb Mortl, could see his sophisticated sense of color and composition. She observed his creative and social development grow substantially as well. His classmates were in awe of how he translated his vision onto canvas.

He loved his friends and teachers in his special ed classroom. Even though he was good at reading and spelling, math was more of a challenge.

I didn't see any reason for him to integrate into regular education classes. I knew he would be bored because it was beyond his level, and he would become a distraction to others. We wanted him to grow in *his*…the classes where he could use his creativity. He took painting, sewing, drawing, 2D, 3D, graphic design, and ceramics. The beauty of art is that you keep creating, learning new techniques, and opening your mind to explore and perfect your style. All of the creativity was giving life to Caleb. We are committed to making connections in his brain. Creating art does this for him.

Circle of Love

No Fear of Failure

Caleb isn't held back by fear of failure. If he wants to learn how to do something, Google and YouTube are his friends. His determination and outlook on life are inspirational. When he was 14 years old, he learned how to tie his first tie—perfect!

State Fair

Caleb's painting of *Younique* was the first time it was apparent to us that he had artistic talent. His teacher, Deb, sent me a picture of his painting and announced that he won 1st place in the Special Needs Category at State Fair. When I saw his painting, I immediately thought of Picasso. To me, it seemed like a cross between Elvis and John Lennon! His lines and color choice were unique and amazing.

Younique

The excitement of placing first quickly went to the next level when he was asked to be a Guest Artist at the State Fair. As parents, excitement and nervousness swelled up the morning of the big day because we wanted everything to be perfect! As always, he sensed the stress and need for perfection and

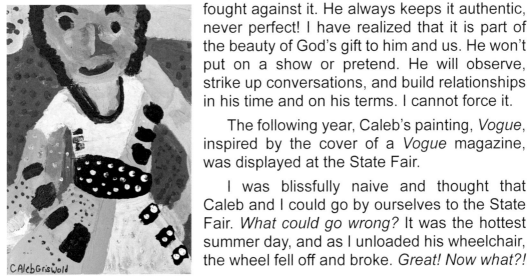

CAlebGrisWold

Vogue

fought against it. He always keeps it authentic, never perfect! I have realized that it is part of the beauty of God's gift to him and us. He won't put on a show or pretend. He will observe, strike up conversations, and build relationships in his time and on his terms. I cannot force it.

The following year, Caleb's painting, *Vogue*, inspired by the cover of a *Vogue* magazine, was displayed at the State Fair.

I was blissfully naive and thought that Caleb and I could go by ourselves to the State Fair. *What could go wrong?* It was the hottest summer day, and as I unloaded his wheelchair, the wheel fell off and broke. *Great! Now what?!*

How can he possibly walk around State Fair? Slowly but surely, Caleb shuffled his way to a parking lot bus that transported us to the main gate. Much to my chagrin but to his delight, I paid for a costly scooter rental, but it was worth every penny. Caleb loved his independence as he maneuvered the scooter with ease, and it was a joy to live in the moment with him. Since I didn't have an agenda, my only job was to keep up with him.

We headed for our car at the end of the sweltering hot day. We had to return the electric scooter, so we both slowly walked to where I thought our car was parked. Complete panic washed over me. *OH, NO! Where is our car?!* The State Fair has multiple parking lots with endless vehicles that stretch for what seemed like miles. We slowly went to the front entrance to tell them about our problem. They directed me in the exact opposite direction. Mad, exhausted, and dripping sweat, I begged for a parking attendant to drive us around to find our car. They didn't seem to care, so we trudged to the opposite end of the parking lot in the beating sun. The parking attendants explained that, unfortunately, we were in the wrong lot AGAIN! By this time, I was throwing a holy fit with swearing, flailing arms, and screaming, "My son has a disability! You have put us on a wild goose chase. He cannot walk!!" To that, Caleb responded, "I don't have a disability. What is my disability?? I can walk, Mom." Talk about total role reversal! Caleb, with his deformed feet and balance issues, never complained and was telling me to calm down and be nice. *Gulp.*

Art Is in the Eye of the Beholder

The beauty of the high school art classes is that The Pink Llama Gallery in downtown Cedarburg hosts art shows to display and sell the student artists' works. Caleb was in his glory, buzzing around with excitement as family and friends gathered to celebrate his first show featuring his painting, *Leapfrog*. Seeing Caleb shining in his strengths with his peers was a moment of thankfulness.

The Little Mini Tiny Show was another joyous gallery night, filled with love  from family and friends, but this time selling his work with local artists. Seeing Caleb's *Fruit of the Spirit* collection and *Hope* being purchased was surreal. Art is indeed in the eye of the beholder. *Love*, which I didn't even think would sell, was purchased right away by someone we didn't know. Once she explained that she saw two people hugging, I always viewed it through that precious lens. Isn't that a little life lesson!

The next day, a customer came in and said, "I want to see the paintings of Caleb Griswold." A few weeks later, a lovely couple from England, who celebrated their tenth wedding anniversary, stopped in and said they liked to pick out one piece of art from the places they travel to, and they chose his painting, *Faithfulness*. I would say that God is faithful!

Islands of Brilliance

In addition to painting, Caleb has an eye for graphic design. An amazing resource, Islands of Brilliance, in Milwaukee, is on the cutting edge of graphic design opportunities for neurodiverse individuals.

Caleb's graphic design *Fetch* was selected as their Colectivo coffee label for their fundraiser, so he was honored to be a Guest Artist at their Gallery Night.

It was interesting to see how social Caleb was initially, wanting "his crew" of family and friends to arrive before he started his painting. He greeted everyone while we set up to make it easier to transition into painting.

Once he got into painting mode, we asked him questions, but he didn't answer us anymore. He was in a different mindset. He tuned us out and started his painting. He sweat as his tongue contorted, and he made raspberries with his lips… He was in "the zone."

He had a picture outlined to paint. He painted for about 20 minutes and then walked away to wash his paintbrush. While he was gone, a little boy understandably thought it was an open canvas and started to paint a green squiggly line in the background. Caleb returned and exclaimed, "A boy is going to help me paint." He wasn't flustered or upset; he

changed course and happily proceeded to paint a completely different abstract painting.

That evening, Caleb met a new friend, Tom, from iHeartRadio, who was so touched by his exchange with Caleb. As Caleb walked to the sink, with his paintbrush still in hand, Caleb paused and greeted Tom, "Excuse me, sir, would you like a cup of coffee?" He set down his paintbrush and poured Tom a cup of coffee. "Would you like cream in your coffee?" Tom later interviewed Caleb and me and made a podcast sharing his thoughtful encounter.

For being an obsessive personality, we are always amazed how Caleb can pivot quickly and flit and flutter around a room. We can learn a lot from how he doesn't worry about the small things.

Self-Determination Conference

With the excitement of Caleb's talent emerging, his art teacher, Deb, encouraged me to have his paintings printed on greeting cards. The enthusiasm for his greeting cards was contagious. When we were at my niece's birthday party, a graphic design business owner was visibly touched and bought all the cards we had. Seeing his response was just the encouragement and prompting we needed from the Lord to keep going.

We decided to sell Caleb's art at the upcoming Self-Determination Conference. At the very least, I knew it might provide some great connections. Our first booth—it was getting exciting!

My creative friend, Amie, brainstormed with me to make his booth look welcoming, artsy, and official with our new card racks. Not knowing what to expect, my sister Brenda, Caleb, and I woke up early and drove to Wisconsin Dells. About halfway there, I looked at the schedule again and realized we would be two hours late! I misunderstood the setup time for the vendor booth viewing time. We were not off to a good start.

Knowing it would be a long day and Caleb needed something to occupy him, I requested a corner booth so he could paint a large abstract painting on his easel. The vibrant red, orange, and purple caught the eye of many.

The response from the guests was immediate and incredibly encouraging as they bought cards and inquired about Caleb's paintings on coffee mugs and tote bags from his Fine Art America website.

To see Caleb "work the crowd" was inspiring. He had no fear, and he was a natural salesman. Since our vendor booth was in the large dining room, he mingled with guests during the breaks, "Do you have a dog? Because I paint dogs. Go talk to my mom. She's right over there." Guests were excitedly showing us their dog pictures and telling us that Caleb had sent them. People texted dog pictures and commissioned him to paint their dogs.

Until that point, he received one request from a neighbor friend to paint their dog. Painting dogs was his favorite subject, but as people commissioned him to paint their dogs at the conference, I wasn't sure how they would turn out. *What were we promising? I know Caleb loves to paint dogs, but would it look like their beloved pet?*

Following the conference, his new friends were following through for their commissioned pet portraits. One was even for a pair of cats! He has never painted a cat. Now it has to look like their own! God has a funny sense of humor. Caleb didn't feel any pressure. His response was always the same, "Of course, I can paint that," and proceeded to paint strokes without hesitation. I told people they were not obligated to buy them because we had no idea how they would turn out. The progress in his skills has been steady and remarkable, but some of his first portraits are the most endearing.

Smudge and Gary

Arts for All

An amazing contact we made during the Self-Determination Conference was Arts for All in Madison, Wisconsin. They were a catalyst for Caleb to seek self-employment as an artist. Their mission is "to expand the capabilities, confidence, and quality of life for children and adults with disabilities by providing programs in dance, drama, creative writing, music, and visual art." As advocates for people with disabilities, they could see that Caleb had the vital qualities to be successful. He is a natural salesman who connects with people. He has a painting talent with his whimsical, colorful style, family support, and dog portrait niche. God was working, and it was another confirmation that we were on the right path.

Caleb's dog portrait, *Zoe*, received the Creative Power Award. This meant it was part of a Traveling Exhibit that traveled to libraries, galleries, and public buildings throughout the state for three years.

Our relationship with Arts For All continues to be a source of encouragement. Two people contacted us after seeing Caleb's artwork. First,

Zoe

David Rettig from OvaInnovations, a pet food ingredient company, reached

out to say that while his wife was at a hospital in Madison, he saw some of Caleb's paintings. He was so moved by his work and wanted to buy some paintings for his headquarters. It was wonderful to meet his family and team at Caleb's studio, and they commissioned him to paint their employees' dog portraits for their new offices. Caleb's waiting list added 13 more dogs that day!

A second touching email came from Jeff Meyer:

Caleb,
I was at the Arts For All gallery show in Madison to see a piece of art my daughter submitted for the same show where you had a display of a couple of pieces that I fell in love with. One was a Holstein cow, and

the other was a red barn. Although it was not for sale, I was wondering if you would consider selling the one or both to display in my office. If they are not available I would love to commission you for a similar "rural life" piece. Please let me know if you are interested.

Bessie

Thanks,

Jeff R Meyer
Meyer Buildings, Inc.

Laura,
I would commission Caleb for another red barn if he is interested as well. Just a little background on my intentions…I own a construction company that builds rural buildings. Horse barns, dairy barns, pole sheds, etc. My daughter has been diagnosed with Asperger's and debilitating anxiety. Her artwork submitted to this show has prompted me to create an art wall displaying scenes of rural life that speak of what we do and has been created by the talent of others who have physical

and mental challenges. Caleb's painting of "Bessie" pushed me over the edge that night and now I'm so excited to put it together. So if you are OK with it, I would be grateful to come meet Caleb when it works for you but totally understand if you are not comfortable with that too. Just know he is so talented and has sparked a chord with me as I'm sure he has done with others!! I can't wait to take this project to the next level!

Talk to you soon.
Jeff Meyer

Meyer Buildings

Picture It!

When Caleb was in high school, he was excited to be in the homecoming parade with his classmates and their Best Buddies. I misread the time he needed to be there, so I raced to get him to the fairgrounds. Unfortunately, I took a wrong turn, making us even later. I contacted his teacher over the phone, but we missed his class since the parade was moving. The road was closed for the parade. I was ready to let it go, but I could see that the parade's end was within walking distance. I pulled over and Caleb jumped out and scooted as fast as his legs could carry him. He caught up to the swim team with the bulldog mascot as the tail end. Shockingly, Caleb, who has difficulty walking long distances, was on such an adrenaline rush. He walked the entire length of downtown Cedarburg with the swim team. He waved and hugged his friends along the whole way. I quickly ran ahead to find him at the end of the parade when he turned the corner towards the school, but I could not find him. He was no longer with the parade. Searching frantically, someone said they saw him picked up by the policeman. Pretty soon, he called me to say that I should let Jesse, who was also in the parade with his hockey team, know that when Jesse saw him in the police car, he wasn't being arrested. The policeman was taking him to school!

Chapter Resources:

Fine Art America
Caleb Griswold Art – Fine Art America
www.fineartamerica.com/profiles/caleb-griswold

Islands of Brilliance
www.islandsofbrilliance.org

Self-Determination Conference
www.wi-bpdd.org/index.php/wisconsin-self-determination-conference

Arts for All
Artist Profile - Caleb Griswold
www.youtube.com/watch?v=BTDX0kPQps4
www.artsforallwi.org

 Scan here to watch!

Advocating

For it is God who works in you to will and
to do according to His good purpose.
Philippians 2:13

Advocating for your child takes work, commitment, and tenacity. As a teacher and a parent of a special needs child, I know that the collaboration between the teacher and the parent is extremely valuable. I prepared for IEP (Individualized Education Plan) meetings using the information I gathered from Caleb's physical therapist, Barb Hypes, who profoundly understood Caleb. At times, the IEP discussions were stressful and tense, but it was essential to have open communication and offer insight. When the partnership was strong, the insight, tips, and suggestions were received as helpful.

Seeing Caleb's art talent, I wanted him to take as many art classes as possible. Since the IEP team and I had differing ideas on the classes for him to take as a special education student, the high school and I mutually agreed to include a mediator on our IEP team. The Wisconsin Special Education Mediation System helps parents and schools work together to resolve disputes about special education.

Spring Has Sprung

Including a mediator as part of the IEP team is sometimes necessary; it is why these organizations are in place. I was glad we went this route. It allowed us to keep the relationship with the school strong, articulate our desires, feel heard, and include a team of people to brainstorm more options for scheduling.

In preparation for the Mediated IEP, I created a video highlighting Caleb's life skills and accomplishments. I didn't know how to create an iMovie, but I sat at the kitchen table from 10 a.m. to 10 p.m. to figure it out. It only seemed like a few hours. I was completely engrossed in my mission; now, it is a valuable keepsake. Sometimes pictures can convey what words cannot.

Chapter Resources:

Caleb's Resumé Video
www.youtu.be/8HKUwTmwmfQ

 Scan here to watch!

Wisconsin Special Education Mediation System
www.wsems.us

Silos of Talent

The heart of the discerning acquires knowledge,
for the ears of the wise seek it out.

Proverbs 18:15

I was not afraid to seek counsel and opportunities for Caleb. Some connections did not lead to anything, but it was necessary to keep pressing. One contact that turned out to be exceptional was the Treffert Center. The Treffert Center invites families "to explore the potential of the human mind, focusing on strengths rather than limitations."

We filled out a 70+ page application for Caleb to be a patient at the Treffert Center. Following the neuropsychological assessment, the doctor concluded and confirmed what we knew—he doesn't have autism but autistic tendencies. His IQ is 44, whereas the average IQ for an 18-year-old is 105.

By God's grace, we had the privilege of meeting Dr. Darold Treffert. He was 80+ years old and retired, but he agreed to come in and meet with us regarding Caleb's artistic talent.

Dr. Treffert, the guru of autism, had worked closely with several savants, including Kim Peek, Leslie Lemke, and Temple Grandin.

Kim Peek was the inspiration for *Rain Man*. Surprisingly, Kim Peek didn't have autism; he had Agenesis of the Corpus Callosum, the same diagnosis as Caleb. He, too, was highly obsessive and had difficulty understanding personal space and wanted to hug too tightly. Eventually, he learned what was appropriate, but it took many years of reminders and training.

Knowing that Caleb's physical therapist, Barb Hypes, modeled her therapy after Temple Grandin, we were thrilled to have the opportunity to have a consultation with him.

We knew that Caleb didn't have autism, nor was he a savant, but I wanted to know how to properly advocate for him and his artistic talent as he entered adulthood.

With his warm, gentle personality, Dr. Treffert opened by asking what I wanted to know. I asked, "Now what? Now that Caleb is 18 and almost ready to graduate high school, where do we go from here?"

He said, "Train his talent." Here are some takeaways from the valuable conversation we shared:

- Pursue organizations that work with individuals who have autism
- Continue to train his talent in the arts, especially in painting. Pursuing

this avenue will open up opportunities for him. See where it leads. At the very least, it builds valuable qualities, including self-esteem

- Caleb has "silos of talent that stand in contrast to his IQ." I thought that was a brilliant way of wording it. It describes Caleb perfectly. His silos include art, dogs, and the elderly

- He said to find an art mentor for him to work 1:1. Caleb needs someone who understands obsessions and knows how to teach painting

Sadly, Dr. Treffert died several years after we met him. We are grateful to God for his significant impact on Caleb and the direction we went based on his wise counsel.

Buckley

Chapter Resource:

Treffert Center
www.ssmhealth.com/treffert-center

Paradigm Shift

*Stand firm then, with the belt of truth buckled around your waist,
with the breastplate of righteousness in place, and with your feet
fitted with the readiness that comes from the gospel of peace. In
addition to all this, take up the shield of faith, with which you can
extinguish all the flaming arrows of the evil one. Take the helmet of
salvation and the sword of the Spirit, which is the word of God.*

Ephesians 6:14-17

Sometimes people can say things out of fear and concern that send you to a dark place. The natural inclination is to fear the worst. My mind could quickly go to the worst scenario every time, the *what if...* This is why we need to rely on the Lord to carry us through the journey. Fear can consume us if we do not wear God's complete armor daily. We are open to being proactive and doing all we can to guard Caleb against harm. The reality is that we do not know what will happen in his life. Below is a guttural response that rose up from my toes regarding someone's comment about Caleb's behavior. Of course, we see his behaviors, and we are concerned. To think we don't is extremely insulting.

We Choose

Yes, we see his behaviors.
We know them better than anyone else. We live them.
We live them every day, every night.
All day, every day, 24 hours a day, 7 days a week,
long before you came into his life and long after you leave.
We have lost friendships and severed relationships over this issue.

We see exactly what you are seeing
and an unbelievable amount more than you will ever know or be able to understand.

You may not be able to wrap your head around this paradigm shift,
but we choose to see it as an obsession
rather than oppositional, naughty, stubborn, or manipulative behavior.

At three years old, Caleb's renowned therapist told us,
"You will be teachers and advocates for Caleb for a lifetime.
You will need to teach others how to work with Caleb for the rest of his life."
I didn't understand the depth of that truth at the time.

As parents,
our approach is to anticipate a meltdown, avoid a meltdown,
distract, redirect, negotiate,
and plan accordingly.

We choose to get into his mind and try to understand what it must be like to be him,
trying to bring order to his chaotic world.

His shining, creative, caring, helpful moments far outweigh his emotional outbursts.

We do not correct every behavior or see every behavior as a teachable moment.
This would exasperate him and steal our joy.

Caleb is a work in progress, given over to God daily.
We don't know his future,
but today, we choose to look at his strengths
and develop those rather than focus on his behaviors.

Celebrating 18 Years

"For I know the plans I have for you," declares the Lord, "plans to prosper you and not to harm you, plans to give you hope and a future."

Jeremiah 29:11

When Caleb turned 18, our lives changed. He transitioned from Children's Long Term Support to Aging and Disability Resource Center (ADRC). We became guardians of Caleb, and our funding changed to IRIS (Include, Respect, I Self-Direct), a state program for special needs waiver funding.

Through IRIS, Caleb has a budget from which Andy and I receive money for Personal Care and Supportive Home Care. Caleb receives a budget for Shared Ride taxi, workouts, mileage, art classes, and respite care. We are grateful for this needed support.

After much research, filling out applications, and waiting for approvals, Independence First, an organization that offers home modifications for individuals with disabilities, came to our house for an evaluation. It was determined that it was unsafe for him to straddle the bathtub by holding on to the soap dish handle. He needed a walk-in shower with a bench. It was a huge blessing to have a new, safe shower. The plan was to have Andy complete the rest of the bathroom renovation. One day, long before Andy felt inspired, Caleb decided to start the demolition because his ceramics teacher collected tiles for the mosaic projects. He was anxious to give her our outdated peach tiles.

A Perfect Day

Caleb's graduation was a perfect day. It was a proud milestone to see him honored for being one of three people who had put in over 900 hours of volunteering while in high school. Caleb entertained himself by bobbing his head and playing with his tassel during the ceremony. He walked across the stage and handed his diploma to Grandma Johnson as he had lovingly promised her. Conquering Caleb had achieved beyond expectations.

It seemed only fitting for Caleb to hand out his invitations to his graduation celebration. Over 100 people celebrated with us, including our family and friends, Caleb's friends from Muttland Meadows, the nursing home, church,

teachers, caretakers, and job coache. My friend Amie helped decorate it like a wedding; Uncle Gregg brought his smoker at 3 a.m. and served brisket while my sister Brenda and dear friend, Lori *(on right in the photo)*, bustled around attending to every detail. We were filled with great joy to see the laughter as guests gathered under the tent with church pews on a beautiful sunny day. The guests toured Caleb's "art gallery" downstairs and purchased his greeting cards. Caleb was in his glory and loved having "his people" celebrate with him!

Caleb often asked us when he would get his driver's license. We excitedly told him that he would get his lawn mower's license. With his graduation money, he received new wheels, not a car, but a lawn mower.

Train His Talent

Caleb graduated with his senior class when he was 18 years old, but students with special needs can stay in the transition program until they are 21. Typically taking a life skills class is the appropriate curriculum for transition students. Since he basically runs our household, we knew we didn't want him to receive life skills classes. Caleb is a homemaker who loves to clean and organize—it is his passion! Before he goes to bed, he puts in a load of laundry and loads the dishwasher. We are usually in bed, and he opens our door to say good night when he is done.

Our desire was for continued art instruction during the transition program. The advice from Dr. Treffert is what drove me to advocate. Since God began to open doors for Caleb's art business, we were pretty confident that we were going to pursue an art business for him. We were not sure how his business would grow, but we could see it naturally unfolding.

For this reason, I didn't want life skills classes for Caleb. I knew he would be a behavior problem if he felt micromanaged. I wanted him to receive all of the art instruction at high school he could receive because the bond and connection that he had with his art teachers was undeniable. He was flourishing under their tutelage.

We are grateful that his art teacher, Deb Mortl *(on right in the photo below)*, continued to be his advocate. As an art therapist, she could see the creative and technical levels Caleb was presenting and knew how to work with his unique character and skill set. As a professional artist, she provided him with opportunities to exhibit and sell his work. Caleb enjoys participating in gallery and art events. Attending painting and graphic design classes for another year would afford him the opportunity to continue with these events that he may not be able to pursue on his own. I knew the social skills he acquired in a studio class would also teach him responsibility, accountability, and time management.

His drawing and 2D art teacher, Chris Behrs, observed that Caleb interacted well with the high school students. Since he does not do well with micromanaging, the higher-level independent art classes were a good option. Mr. Behrs would assign a project and had a thought of what he was expecting. He watched Caleb drawing and drawing and couldn't see it coming together at all, and then all of a sudden, Caleb created his own way to have his pop-up 2D art. Caleb's brain is firing; he is creative and goes about it differently than most people.

Caleb's ceramics teacher, Julie Grisar *(on left in the photo above)*, was in awe of his progression and talent. When he first started in ceramics, Caleb's paraprofessional needed to provide hand-over-hand assistance. In just a few short years, he was grasping the techniques independently. After high school, she encouraged Caleb to pursue ceramics because she believed his whimsical style was marketable.

Advocating is a continuous and sometimes contentious journey, but why wouldn't we want to pursue it for Caleb? Isn't that what every parent wants for their child? To see their gifts develop and help foster them? We knew he was not going to go to college. We shadowed an art class at a technical college; he wasn't at their level, and the instruction exceeded his comprehension. His passion is art, and the art instruction he was already receiving was his "least restrictive environment."

Since he didn't fit the mold of a traditional transition program student, it was a mutual decision with the school to continue to have a mediator on his IEP team. It led to more advocating, researching his options, and, most importantly, thinking outside the box to meet Caleb's unique needs.

One critical resource I discovered while preparing for Caleb's transition program goals was an advocate from Wisconsin Disabilities. The valuable information I gained from those conversations gave me hope. She spoke my language and affirmed that asking for things other than the traditional program is acceptable. She explained what Caleb's "least restrictive environment" could be and suggested appropriate goals for him.

There were hard conversations with the IEP team during this time, but I believe we all grew from working this out, and hopefully, it blazed a trail for other students in the transition program.

Chapter Resources:

Aging and Disability Resource Center of Ozaukee County
www.co.ozaukee.wi.us/442/Long-Term-Care

IRIS
www.dhs.wisconsin.gov/iris/index.htm

Independence First
www.independencefirst.org

Wisconsin Disabilities
www.disabilityrightswi.org

Budding Artist

The Lord your God is with you, the Mighty Warrior who saves.
He will take great delight in you; in His love He will no longer
rebuke you, but will rejoice over you with singing.

Zephaniah 3:17

The Pink Llama

We were thrilled when Tammie, the owner of The Pink Llama in downtown Cedarburg, invited Caleb to sell his cards at her store. It was quite an honor that he was recognized as a legitimate artist, not because of his special needs but because of his whimsical artistic style. It was inclusion at its finest. He was beginning to build relationships with many different artists and customers. They appreciated his personality and work, and his story added significant meaning to his art. Other doors opened when Tammie allowed Caleb to have his booth in front of The Pink Llama at Cedarburg's Strawberry Festival, Wine and Harvest Festival, and this year, he was in the Winter Festival.

Pink Llama

The Arts Mill

Caleb participated in the 24-Hour Show at the Arts Mill Gallery & Boutique, so I had to pick up his canvases. After walking around the bustling studio space, the welcoming director, Paula, explained that artists rent and have access to their studio space 24/7 to create and sell art. Since it is a co-op art studio, artists volunteer some hours in addition to renting their studio. She informed me, "We have one tiny space left." Immediately, I knew it was precisely what he needed—a little space to paint where there are other artists for friendships and peace of mind for safety.

We were eager to get him settled into his new studio space, so we loaded his things onto the freight elevator built in 1884. Unaware there was a light, I rode the creaky elevator in the dark, so excited about this new opportunity.

It is touching to see the artist community embrace Caleb. His art studio allows him independence and a place to socialize and create art. He loves to visit his friends at the coffee shop and bar on the first floor, especially since dogs are welcome.

Empty Containers

Of course with Caleb, some sticky situations arise. He tries to help, but his obsession with cleaning empty containers gets him in trouble.

> *Artists:*
>
> *I am opening up at the Mill and have walked in to find the sink in a horrible state. It is as though pots of dirt were thrown down it?? There is dirt on the floor, counter, in the sink–which is completely backed up with dirt. There are containers floating in the sink.*
>
> *I know we all break things/make mistakes, but it's best to know about them so we can fix them instead of "find them" when you walk in. Whoever is responsible needs to bring in Drano, and let's hope that helps the situation.*
>
> *You can write in confidence and not the group.*

> *Bummed,*
> *Paula DeStefanis*

Caleb quickly replied to the entire group:

> *so sorry Paula it was me I didn't mean to do it I will try to fix it when i get to the arts mill today so my apologies*
>
> Caleb😹😹😿🙀😧

In an effort to clean, he sometimes makes an enormous mess! Knowing he couldn't miss his Shared Ride taxi that day, he left abruptly. As I read the email, I knew it was Caleb and that Andy needed to do an emergency run. Having open communication with Paula has been helpful because Caleb doesn't always understand boundaries and housekeeping rules.

Artist-in-Residence

When Caleb was 20 years old, he was excited to be the Artist-in-Residence at the Cedarburg Cultural Center. His work was displayed for guests to view

and purchase for one month. He was in his glory every weekend, greeting his friends and making new ones. Guests also saw the artist at work when he felt inspired to paint his large abstract painting on his easel.

Chapter Resources:

The Pink Llama Gallery
www.thepinkllama.com/

The Arts Mill
www.theartsmill.org/artists/caleb-griswold/

Navigating a Pandemic

So do not fear, for I am with you, do not be dismayed, for I am your God.
I will strengthen you and help you;
I will uphold you with My righteous right hand.
Isaiah 41:10

Prior to the 2020 pandemic, Caleb loved to go to Village Pointe Commons, an independent senior living community, to play with Grandma Johnson every Saturday. They would do puzzles, play Double Solitaire, and Caleb watched her sew. At 4 p.m., they went down to eat dinner in the dining room. As a social butterfly, he sat with old and new friends weekly.

Part of the after dinner routine was for residents to get their mail. Wanting to be helpful, Caleb began wrapping many spiral keychains around his arm as he brought their mail to them at the dining room table. Again, he was in his glory, using his gifts to bless the elderly, and they responded to him with gratitude and delight.

Navigating a pandemic is difficult for everyone. The thought of navigating it with Caleb drained every ounce of energy from me. Caleb thrives on having his days scheduled with weekly activities seven days a week, 24 hours a day. *What will we do with him now that everything has come to a screeching halt?!*

Trust me; it was not easy. My patience ran very thin every day. However, God graciously walked us through that time. School and the volunteer opportunities at the Humane Society and LaSata Nursing Home ended, but he didn't skip a beat in finding other ways to live. I loved when he got himself into a creative project. Often, it meant that he created a big mess, but I didn't mind because he was happy and occupied for hours on end.

He made signs to spread some love at Village Pointe. "Hi, Grandma and friends! I miss you all because of the bad virus season. Love Caleb and Xander" and "Honk and wave & say hi to Village Pointe friends."

Balcony Choir

We saw on the news that the activities director had a balcony choir at Village Pointe Commons. Since the senior living facility was on lockdown, she invited

all residents out on their balconies as she stood outside in the middle of the courtyard to lead a sing-along of their childhood jingles, patriotic songs, and hymns. When she invited the public to join them, Caleb jumped on that invitation. He joined the balcony choir every day at 4 p.m. for several months. Since it was spring, it was still cold, but that didn't stop him. Eventually, as it got warmer, he rode his bike, with Xander running alongside him.

Unfortunately, the activities director became sick and could no longer attend, so Caleb became the choir director. The residents had a songbook and would yell down the page number of the song they wanted to sing.

He also created his songbook binder. He spent his afternoon googling songs to sing, making copies, and assembling them in his plastic binder. Their favorite daily singing request was "How Much Is That Doggie in the Window." When they wanted to give something to him, such as a basket with candy, they lowered it down with a rope. Since he knew all the residents from getting their mail and eating dinner with them, he called them by name to see how they were doing. Since the residents were isolated and could not have visitors in the building, this heartfelt gesture amplified their love for Caleb.

From the Heart

Another of Caleb's pastimes during the pandemic was sewing masks. He did these all by hand by cutting the dog print fabric, putting hair ribbons on the ends for the ears, and hand stitching each mask. He took orders when he called his friends on Messenger. They were not the most elegant masks, with frayed edges and uneven material, but his heart was in the right place.

© Edwin Gonzalez

Whimsical Art

Caleb and I also gathered driftwood from the shores of Lake Michigan. He began painting whimsical driftwood for planters and decorations—another addition to his art offerings.

While Caleb had his virtual ceramics class during COVID-19, I saw the artist at work. When his tongue was working it, I knew he was "in the zone." His tenacity and perseverance were impressive. To make a three-legged vase, he firmly rolled out the clay, scratched hatch marks with his scoring tool, formed it into a cylinder, and sealed the seam. It collapsed. Again he firmly rolled out the clay, scratched hatch marks with his scoring tool, formed it into a cylinder, and sealed the seam. It collapsed again. By the third time, I tried to hold part of it to make it easier for him so it didn't collapse again. Frustrated, he said, "Mom, the video only shows two hands, not four!" I knew to back away and let him figure it out. He did not give up, and I was impressed with his artistic muscles and determination.

Cemetery Ministry

Grandma Johnson and Caleb brought flowers to Grandpa's grave in the spring. Caleb took it upon himself to water flowers daily. If Grandpa's flowers didn't need it, a whole cemetery full of flowers did. Lovingly and dutifully, Caleb rode his bike to the cemetery daily, with Xander running alongside him. He would water the flowers, pull weeds, pray for the people at the cemetery, dust off the grass clippings, throw away dead Christmas wreaths, and even attend services.

With the sincerest heart, he would text me throughout the day.

"I was just at someone's funeral service today, and it just ended. Do you want me to stay here or come home?"

"Xander and I are at cemetery school today."

"What do you mean?" I texted.

"We are watering all the flowers, and we are memorizing all of their names!"

God ever so gently prepared Caleb for Grandma Johnson's passing. Since they were so close and her health deteriorated quickly, caretaking at the cemetery was comforting.

Sadly, the day came when I had to tell him Grandma Johnson had passed.

Sympathetically, I whispered, "Caleb, I am sorry to say this, but Grandma has passed away."

Immediately he said, "I'm going to delete her contact information on my phone." In shock, I told him to save them, but he had already deleted her phone number and text messages.

As shocking and insensitive as it seemed, I knew I needed to let him process his dear Grandma's death as he needed to. Later, a friend with a special needs child said her son did the same thing. It makes sense to me that in his mind, Caleb knew Grandma was in heaven. He would not see her anymore; therefore, there was no need to keep her contact information here on earth.

Grandma's Funeral

For God so loved the world that He gave His one and only Son,
that whoever believes in Him will not perish but have eternal life.
John 3:16

Caleb spoke at Grandma Johnson's funeral. He began with her favorite verse, John 3:16. Completely comfortable at the microphone, he shared his heart and love for his grandma. In the closing of his speech, he read, "I always called my grandma to check in at 10 a.m. and 9 p.m. When it was a full moon, we always looked at Grandpa's moon. Now she is looking at Grandpa's moon from heaven. As we said every night, 'Sweet dreams, Grandma.' I love you and will miss you. Have fun with Jesus!"

The Power of Love

A sweet friendship refreshes the soul.

Proverbs 27:9

I saw an advertisement requesting artwork for the upcoming edition of *Cedarburg Bridge* magazine, so I submitted *Diva*. It led to us being the featured family for June 2021 *Cedarburg Bridge*. It was another opportunity to share how God turned a devastating diagnosis into something miraculous.

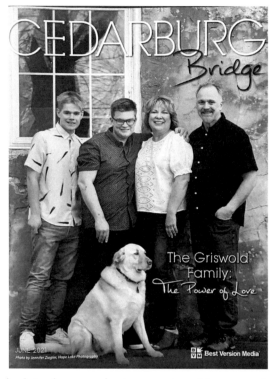

Volunteer of the Year

Overjoyed, Caleb was selected to receive an Ozaukee Impact Award - Volunteer of the Year. We wanted everything to go smoothly and look like we had it all together for this memorable event. However, he is on his terms, in his time, and does not seek to impress anyone. Caleb needed to be ready to receive his award and give a speech when his category was introduced. The luncheon was first, and since he was mingling with others, he didn't start to eat until the ceremony began. Knowing he sometimes froze with surprises, we told him a few days prior that he was chosen and needed to give a speech. As the

emcee introduced the Volunteer of the Year nominees, Caleb didn't stand but rather continued to eat. We knew they would call his name any minute, so we all frantically tried to take away his turkey wrap. Across the table, my sister made a deal with him to have her cookie afterward, but nothing worked! I was giving him the desperate "CALEB" eyes. He looked at me with chipmunk cheeks bulging with a turkey wrap, mayonnaise oozing down his face, and muttered, "Hmm??" They called his name. He hesitated a moment and went up and nailed the speech! Sometimes we want things to be picture-perfect, but why do we fret? Caleb is about as authentic as one can be.

This picture captures the deep connection felt between Caleb and David. Miraculously, we met David when I was looking for safe environments for Caleb to hang out with his friends. We stopped by to visit Caleb's "showering guy" Tim, who worked for Balance, a community based adult day care near our house. Tim wasn't there, but after inquiring about adult day care, the staff told us about a room where David hung out with his friends. David is blind and has a seeing-eye dog, Max. There was great joy in the room as David, Max, and his friends gathered, shared meals, played video games, and just hung out with each other. It was touching that David and Max surprised Caleb by attending the luncheon when he heard Caleb was receiving the award.

Mel's Charities

The recipient of Volunteer of the Year is to choose an organization to receive a donation. Caleb immediately chose Mel's Charities, an amazing organization in Ozaukee County. Caleb formed a close friendship with the

director of Mel's Charities, Tom Stanton, and his wife, Nancy, while at Muttland Meadows. Mel's Charities mission has "a strong emphasis on special needs, memorial scholarships, and human service organizations." They are currently building Northern Gateway, a multi-generational campus with housing for individuals with disabilities, recreation venues, meaningful job opportunities, and, Caleb's favorite, an art studio. We are in awe of God's provision and timing regarding the calling on Tom's life through Mel's Charities to gracefully meet the needs of the special needs community.

A Pastor's Heart

Caleb has a pastor's heart. Seeing him so eager to study his Bible, attend church, and love people freely is a delight.

Like Grandma Just, he has a deep desire to study his Bible. He will spread out all of his Bibles, highlighters, journals, and devotionals on the kitchen table. It is soothing to my soul to see him sit for hours and fastidiously find the right books of the Bible, chapters, and verses, highlight and copy them

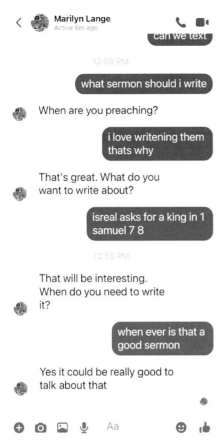

word for word in his journal. He excitedly reads them aloud, stumbling over difficult words. Caleb read God's promise to me this morning with all sincerity and authority.

I am with you and will watch over you wherever you go, and I will bring you back to this land. I will not leave you until I have done what I have promised you. Genesis 28:15

During a sermon, Caleb is attentive as he writes many pages of notes in his journal. The notes don't necessarily reflect what the pastor said, but his heart is in the right place, and the Word of God penetrates deep into his soul. He usually sits in the front row, and we can only see his broad shoulders because he is bending his head to take notes. If the pastor goes too fast, he takes a picture to enlarge it on his phone.

Caleb spends hours rewriting his sermon notes, and he has texted several of our pastor friends to see if they will teach him how to write a sermon. God has a plan for his life and uses him in ways we will only understand when we get to heaven. Andy and I desire to foster an environment for him to grow in his faith.

> i want to be a paster so badly and pray for people can you please train me

5:42 PM

I can try to help

> do i have to fill out a form

How do you mean?

> to be a paster

Sent 21m ago

God Moments

When Caleb was about 13 years old, we were at church when he excitedly came barreling toward his grandma friend for a hug. She motioned for him to slow down and asked, "Would you like to escort me to the prom?" Caleb and this lovely lady locked arms, and he walked her to her car. She blew him a kiss, and he blew one back to her.

He approached a lady at church and said, "You look stressed out," and he prayed for her. She later told me that he is intuitive and can break down the barriers with people who would not usually reach out for prayer.

We were part of a close-knit Bible study class at church. Caleb always had something to share with the group, so the teacher devoted 5-10 minutes to "Caleb time." It was heartwarming to see mutual love exchanged. One Sunday, during the worship service, he scooted in between the Bible study teacher and his wife. He lifted his arms, hugged both, and kept his arms around them. They swayed as they worshiped the Lord together.

Chapter Resource:

Mel's Charities
www.melscharities.org

Communication Breakdown

I will give you hidden treasures, riches stored in secret places,
so that you may know that I am the Lord, the God of Israel,
who summons you by name.
Isaiah 45:3

Literally Literal

Growing up, my favorite children's book was <u>Amelia Bedelia</u> because she reminded us of our favorite "life of the party" Aunt Emelie. Like Amelia Bedelia, Caleb often interprets what he hears in terms of the literal meanings of words.

Caleb was really into baking carrot oatmeal muffins. After doing several batches with him, he was on his own. He began taking orders on a sign-up sheet for his Village Pointe and Bible study friends. The recipe says to turn halfway through baking. He was literally turning each little muffin halfway around.

I ended up in the emergency room due to heart palpitations and elevated blood pressure. That night as Caleb took my temperature and tucked me into bed, he said, "Mom, next time you have a heart attack, could you have it on a Tuesday because that way, when I am working at St. Mary's, I can just stop and see you."

When Caleb was seven years old, he had the flu. As he was throwing up, he pleaded, "Pray for me!" A few minutes later, he repeated, "Pray for me!" The third time, he lifted his head and asked, "Mommy, what are you praying because I don't feel any better!"

One Thanksgiving, we invited some friends over for dinner. Our friends brought a vegetable platter with carrot sticks, pea pods, and cherry tomatoes, creating feathers of a turkey. We enjoyed conversing for a while and then announced it was time to eat the turkey dinner. Bewildered, Caleb commented, "I thought this was the turkey." He had been quietly cutting his "turkey" carrot sticks into bite-size pieces.

Sometimes we need to talk in code. I told a friend that someone was wearing a patch to quit smoking. Since the conversation was in front of Caleb, I said, "He had a patch on his jeans." Caleb quickly responded, "Oh, well, tell him to give his jeans to me; I sew. I can sew his jeans for him."

When Caleb's hair gets long, he says, "I need a haircut; it's getting wiggy!"

When Caleb lost me in a store, he would have me paged. It became relatively common to hear my name over the loudspeaker. One day, I heard, "Would Diane please come to the front." I thought, 'Wow, for once, it isn't me!' After they called a third time, I decided to check. He was waiting for me to find him. When I asked, "Why didn't you say, 'Laura?'" he said, "I just wanted to see if you would come to Diane."

The Disconnect

Since there is a disconnect between Caleb's chronological age and cognitive age, he can be easily misunderstood. When I shared my heart with Caleb's childhood speech therapist, Chris Anderson, regarding situations where he has been misunderstood, she explained that it is Social Communication Disorder. *Ahh…there is a name for it! Why did it take me this long to realize this?* I think because up until that point, it wasn't a huge problem. Now that he is older and looks "normal," people expect him to be appropriate.

According to the American Speech-Language-Hearing Association (ASHA): "Social Communication Disorder (SCD) is characterized by persistent difficulties with the use of verbal and nonverbal language for social purposes. Primary difficulties may be in social interaction, social understanding, pragmatics, language processing, or any combination of the above.

Social communication encompasses the following components:

- **pragmatics**—communication that focuses on goal-consistent language use in social contexts
- **social interaction**—communication that occurs between at least two individuals
- **social cognition**—an understanding of the mental and emotional states of self and others…expected socially appropriate behavior and consequences of inappropriate behavior
- **language processing**—internal generation of language (expressive), and understanding and interpretation of language (receptive)"

The older Caleb becomes, with his solid build, the more daunting his Social Communication Disorder becomes due to deficiencies in his non-verbal communication (hugging) and ability to read the room.

Caleb gives the tightest bear hugs. Hugging was accepted, and even encouraged, until he got older. Some tried to help him give fist bumps and high fives, but he is a hugger.

Understanding personal space is a common problem for those with SCD because they receive many mixed messages. While Caleb is learning to ask people if they would like a hug, it is usually not what he observes others do, making it more confusing. Others may say "yes," but later change their mind. I teach him that some say "yes" but mean "no." I explain that if he sees people avoiding him, it means "no." Blunt communication is the easiest for him to understand.

Caleb also loves to pray for people. If they agree, he will usually put his hand on their shoulders or hold their hands, bow his head, and say a quick prayer. We have had many difficult conversations trying to teach him to respect boundaries. Yet, we do not want to crush his tender sensitivity to the Holy Spirit in wanting to pray for people.

Some people want prayer and cry when he prays with them. Others cringe. Now that he is older, there is a deeper concern that his gestures of kindness can be easily misunderstood. Even though he has the body of a man, his mind is at a five-year-old level, which can make for awkward social interactions.

I understand that Caleb's lack of boundaries may cause fear or that it can be a trigger for some people. We need to be sympathetic and work towards understanding each other better. As our society works to foster inclusivity, it is important to remember the special needs population longs to be included.

Creating and respecting personal boundaries is needed and healthy. It requires many conversations, sometimes causing misunderstandings and hurt feelings. The ideal situation is when those who feel led, commit to working it through with Caleb until he eventually understands. We appreciate these angels who have come into his life without judgment and teach him personal boundaries while showing respect.

He is making progress in understanding personal boundaries. Still, we continue to pray for wisdom, the hidden treasures of secret places, and a solution we had not thought of before—an answer where only God could make a way.

Social Communication Disorder Card

Chris wisely advised me to create a card with my phone number that Caleb carries in his wallet to explain his Social Communication Disorder to others and to protect him.

My name is Caleb Griswold. I want you to understand that I have a language disorder. My brain processes language differently than other people. It makes talking with you and sometimes understanding your words hard for me. I apologize for using words that offend you or may not make sense. Thank you for being patient with me.

Parking Lot Meltdown

For He will command His angels concerning
you to guard you in all your ways.
Psalm 91:11

The mornings are the most difficult time of the day for Caleb. Getting ready and out the door has always been a problem because he has no concept of time. Before leaving for work, I need to ensure that Caleb is in his taxi. Out of desperation, I assisted him in getting ready.

At times, Caleb gets physical. He gets this way when he is very rattled, clawing for control of any kind. Emotionally, he had been in a bad place for an extended time as we worked with him to respect other people's personal space. He was trying to process, but his brain was in a constant state of chaos. Everything made him irritable and impossible to please. When I tried to help him get dressed, he was bossy and rude, pushing me around and giving orders instead of working with me. He stiff-armed me so I couldn't get past him, and he tensed his body so I couldn't help him. It had been getting progressively worse. One day, I tried to help him make his 7 a.m. taxi, but since I wouldn't help him get ready, he grabbed my leg, and I literally dragged him across the kitchen floor. Steam was coming out of my ears as I made my way out the back door with my disheveled clothes, messy hair, and bleeding toe and calmly told the Shared Ride taxi driver, "I don't think he will make it today."

The following Sunday, I wouldn't help him get ready. I knew helping him no longer worked for me. I had reached my limit, and he knew it. I was going to pick this battle and win. The only way to avoid helping him was to leave. As I made my escape, he tried to muscle me back, but with my adrenaline spiked, I was a pent-up tiger breaking free. Andy was trying to help, but the situation escalated out of control very quickly. It was the coldest day of winter, so in my pajamas, I grabbed whatever coat I could and slid my slippers into Andy's Birkenstocks. I knew Caleb was barreling toward me because he didn't want me to leave. As he and I wrestled at the back door, his elbow went through the glass of the door. I had on my winter coat, so I couldn't feel anything, but Caleb quietly muttered, "Ow."

With my adrenaline still through the roof, I didn't have an ounce of sympathy. I was glad Andy was there to help him; I had to flee. In the freezing cold, with my heels hanging off the edge of the Birks, I stomped up the street. I knew my sister Lynda was on her way to my house because she was going to church with us. As I saw her coming down the street, I vigorously waved my arms, but she drove right past me. I just kept walking. As she entered the house, she immediately sensed the turmoil. Seeing Caleb's head down, she questioned where I was and took off to find me. I was a pathetic sight with freezing tears, dripping snot, slush-soaked slippers, and carrying an exhausted, broken heart. Like a picture of the Holy Spirit, Lynda came racing towards me with her big black truck, swept in, and saved me. I was about as low as I had ever been. She took Caleb for the day so that Andy and I could have some peace. I was worried about his elbow and wanted to take him to the walk-in clinic, but we knew Caleb was deathly afraid and would have another meltdown if we took him. None of us were up for it. Andy and Lynda thought it looked okay when they bandaged him up.

Caleb spent the day having fun at Lynda's house. It was not the right time to punish and lecture him. She strategically tied in conversations about dressing himself, but the goal was to distract him and restore his mental health. Later that night, I planned to pick him up with enough time to go to the walk-in clinic near Lynda's house. He was apologetic, worried if I was okay, and in a good frame of mind. To my surprise, he agreed to go to the clinic and set Google Maps on my phone. As we got closer, he panicked about seeing the doctor, and things turned dreadful. He turned off my Google Maps. I didn't know where I was or how to get home. As we approached the stoplight, I could see the lit Emergency Room sign, so we made it to the parking lot with gentle coaxing.

Caleb freaked out in the empty parking lot and grabbed the steering wheel. He pulled on the wheel in the snow-covered parking lot, and I braced my arms to block him. As we made big circles in the parking lot, all of the motion detector parking lot lights began to go on. Not knowing what to do, I got out of the car but quickly realized he might lock me out in the freezing cold. I got back in and cried. Caleb hates to see me cry—it rocks his world; everything is out of control. But then…God stepped in and gave me the words that resonated with him. "Dad and I cannot care for you when you are like this. You have a choice to make. If you want someone to get you dressed, put your shoes on every day, and do everything for you, they will do that for you in a group home. But if you want to live at home with us, you need to be independent and dress yourself and put on your own shoes. Where would you like to live? In a group home? Or with us?"

With a trembling voice and guard down, he quivered, "I want to live with you guys." I had no idea that he had negative feelings about group homes, but that question helped him turn a corner that day. Sometimes it feels like finding a needle in a haystack, but it is a tremendous relief when you have a drastic breakthrough like that. It is not a gradual change of heart. It is an about-face. I believe it is not naughty, manipulative behavior; it is an obsessive, sensory-charged, fear-driven, out-of-control meltdown. The connection I felt when I watched *Son-Rise: A Miracle of Love* as a little girl still washes over me when there is a breakthrough of this emotional magnitude.

We never made it to the ER, but we made it home safely. A win for today.

Chapter Resource:

American Speech-Language-Hearing Association
www.asha.org/practice-portal/clinical-topics/social-communication-disorder/

Missed Taxi

Caleb's Story Is Still Being Written

Now to Him who can do exceedingly abundantly above all that we ask or think, according to the power that works in us, to Him be glory in the church by Christ Jesus to all generations, forever and ever. Amen.

Ephesians 3:20-21

Restoration

As Caleb and Jesse grew older, their relationship became stronger. They always had a close bond when they were little, but Jesse needed his space. Caleb adored Jesse, but understandably, it was harder for him to understand how to relate to Caleb. Thankfully their relationship evolved from Caleb embarrassing Jesse to Jesse being proud of Caleb.

At the end of Jesse's sophomore year, I happened to go through Jesse's backpack and found a printed PowerPoint presentation. It immediately brought me to tears. The research topic was "Individuals who have persevered despite challenging circumstances." There was a suggested list of actors and athletes, but Jesse decided to research what he knew best, "My Brother."

I don't think he realized how many images and stories would come up when he googled Caleb's name. Since there were several articles and news stories about him, he had a lot of valuable material.

On one slide, Jesse asked, "What can people learn from his life story?" His answer was this:

1. Anything is possible if you put in work
2. People take their walking for granted

Jesse definitely appreciates and admires Caleb's achievements after having a front-row seat to his perseverance. Recently, we ran into the teacher who heard him give the speech that day. She said that the class was pretty rowdy when Jesse, the quietest one in the class, got up in front of all his friends and shared from his heart about his brother. He had the attention of everyone in the room.

When Caleb turned 18, Jesse became a respite care worker for him. The blessing is that Caleb and Jesse spend time together again. One day as they played Xbox, I pressed my ear to the closed door. It warmed my heart to

Dear Jesse

I Love you I shurely do miss you xander is sad your in college and wanted you to stay home I Love your apartment I know you will come home to Visit I Loved going to your hockey games and being the score keeper me and mom are going to madison for Lunch with Jodi me and the cleaning Lady cleaned Your room and your shades and they where dirty and Brown thank you for keeping in touch with me you will get mail tommorrow I Love You Caleb xander

hear Jesse teaching Caleb to play Minecraft together. He was extremely patient and respectful, repeating himself on how to move to the next level. Listening to Jesse's encouragement and understanding with Caleb assured me the close bond would remain.

Jesse understands Caleb and knows how to respond with small rewards. Caleb loves to spend time with Jesse, so telling Caleb that he gets a ride in the front seat of his car when they get ice cream is motivation enough for Caleb to get in the shower and get himself ready. Respite care is a break for us, but to see them interact as brothers is healing.

God restored lost years. All of Jesse's years at the skating rink led to him playing hockey in high school. The grit, determination, and character it developed in Jesse built confidence. While he was at the University of Wisconsin-Milwaukee, he played hockey and later was a hockey team manager. I marvel at God's restoration because I grieved the chaotic years when we could not build special family memories. The hockey games at UWM were an absolute fit because the rink allowed dogs! Caleb was in his glory, and Jesse's teammates embraced Caleb as their biggest fan!

Jesse's Graduation Video:
www.youtube.com/watch?v=K-PYiG7nPLo

Scan here to watch!

A Working Man

Caleb continues to conquer life as a young adult. At 23 years old, he has a very busy schedule, which is just the way he likes it. He works for Aramark

Food Service at Cedarburg High School almost six hours a day, five days a week. He prepares french fries, washes tables, and stacks the dishwasher, which is his favorite. CHS is one of his happy places, so it is fun for him to continue to see his friends.

Thanks A Lot

When Caleb worked at the CHS cafeteria, he was allowed access to food, and his routine at the Arts Mill and the Dollar Tree also included food. Obviously, he was beginning to gain too much weight. Finally, after many conversations about not taking food at the cafeteria, he flipped to a healthy routine. He knew I did not want him to take any more food from the cafeteria. He was doing great with his diet. One day, he missed breakfast, and his taxi was an hour late, so he didn't eat anything until late afternoon. I received a text from Caleb saying, "You let all the lunch ladies and school kids get fat and not me? Thanks a lot. They let me take lunch when I'm at work. Thanks a lot for not feeding your son."

One afternoon a week, he also works at the Dollar Tree stocking the merchandise as straight and orderly as you can imagine! Both jobs work well for him, but some issues have come up. One day, his patient Dollar Tree boss, Tammie, laughed as she told me he stocked all the napkins by the toilet paper. She said, "Now, Caleb, do you wipe your butt with napkins?" He responded, "Well, sometimes!"

He is also learning breakroom refrigerator etiquette. She told him that he could not eat her pizza. She had even taken a bite out of it. He later texted her, *"Hi Tammie it's Caleb I am sorry I ate your pizza that one day I didn't know you like pizza did you see my apology note at Dollar Tree?"*

Your Jeans Fit Me

Caleb took a taxi from his job at Cedarburg High School to his job at Dollar Tree. He was forevermore texting me with confessions, updates, and issues. This one took the cake!

Caleb: Your jeans fit me. Couldn't find mine. Sorry. Is that okay?

Mom: Oh boy, take a picture.

Caleb: No, please. You're going to say no; I just know you. They feel okay. No butt crack showing. Please let me wear them.

We had a good laugh when he came home from work. He was proud of his new look as his chest puffed out like a turkey breast! He definitely didn't need his belt that day. He said his pants were so tight that he couldn't bend his legs in the taxi. The real problem came when he tried to peel himself out of my pants!

Caleb iPhone

Is that look wearied

Yes!! Weird!!

Your jeans fit me couldn't find mine

Sorry

Is that okay?

Oh boy- take a pick

Picture

Read 12:45 PM

No please your going to say no i just know you they feel okay no but crack showing please let me wear them

Friendship Circle - Cafe, Bakery, and Art Studio

God answered our prayer once again in Friendship Circle - Cafe, Bakery, and Art Studio. We heard about their Employment Training Program when Caleb was an Ozaukee County Resource Fair art vendor. As Andy and I were at his booth, Caleb made

his rounds greeting everyone at their booths and telling them he painted dogs. Excited, he introduced us to his new friends, Terry and Eva, from Friendship Circle. Terry spoke my language, "It is easy for some of these young adults to get a job but hard for them to keep it." *Thank you, Lord. This is right where we are with Caleb!*

Caleb was in Employment Training Program, which is a six-month program where he attended two afternoons a week with a small group of bakers who also have special needs. They learned to bake, use kitchen equipment, clean, package the bakery for the cafe, and experience being a barista. While working, the teachers, Chrissie and Eva, incorporated the soft skills of a job, including

teamwork, problem-solving, communication, and time management. The training also included resumé-building, interviewing, and working with companies that embrace individuals with special needs as valuable employees. In addition to the cafe and bakery, the art studio is an added bonus, where he intends to become more involved as time allows. Friendship Circle has become family for Caleb.

Scan here to read the article on Caleb and Friendship Circle!

Paintings and Paws by Caleb, LLC

Since Caleb was in high school, I have been working tirelessly to see if it was viable for him to start his own business, Paintings and Paws by Caleb, LLC. The best way to find out was for him to continue to paint, create art, and sell it. As a beautiful confirmation, Caleb's art is sold at several area stores, online, and at festivals.

Caleb's most significant niche is his commissioned dog portraits. Seeing how he interprets the dog's personality and features is endearing. He captures the reflection of their eyes with vibrancy. He paints cats as well, but his forte is dogs. Since 2018, Caleb has painted over 100 pet portraits, with an ongoing waiting list of over 20. Paintings and Paws by Caleb, LLC, has a Facebook page with side-by-side photos of the

Maya

dog and the painting. It is incredible to see the progression of his skills in just a few years.

We love every minute of seeing Caleb do what he loves. To say it has been an easy endeavor would be a lie. Advocating is never-ending. We would not let the opportunity pass because the challenge of starting his own business was daunting. We dedicated ourselves to advocating throughout his entire life. It is a passion that burns deep inside of me.

Wishek   *Cody*

It began with advocating for his physical needs and moved to advocating for his academic needs through the school system. Now it is advocating for his professional needs with DVR and IRIS programs. The Division of Vocational Rehabilitation (DVR) is "a federal/state program designed to

Jet and Patch

obtain, maintain, and advance employment for people with disabilities by working with DVR consumers, employers, and other partners."

The road less traveled is DVR's Customized Self-Employment. We began with a Feasibility Report. The feedback was a resounding "yes" it is feasible for Caleb to have a profitable and sustainable business for three main reasons—he has a natural talent, a niche with dog portraits, and a supportive family. DVR supplied a lengthy Self-Employment Toolkit of steps to create a DVR-approved business plan. The process moved slowly because it was rarely, if ever, done in Ozaukee County.

After relentless persistence, God graciously sent advocates from other counties. Jeanie Verschay from Employment Connections served as Caleb's Self-Employment Coordinator. Her dedication led to a supportive connection with Anne Hlavacka, the Director of Wisconsin Small Business Development Centers. We shared the vision, determination, and expertise to pull the business plan together. Caleb and I presented our vision virtually to a Business Plan Review Committee of many DVR consultants around Wisconsin.

Paintings and Paws by Caleb, LLC, began as a possibility. However, with a lot of grit, perseverance, and patience, it became a reality. Caleb and I have

an LLC, and the Business Plan Review Committee granted Caleb significant funding for start-up costs.

I wanted to give up many times, but God sent encouragement at the right juncture to uplift, carry, and affirm us to keep moving forward.

Jadda and Jemma

One of those encouraging godsends was Keely Welton, a family friend who agreed to be an art instructor for Caleb. Keely's art and business expertise, coupled with her understanding of Caleb's heart, have taken Paintings and Paws by Caleb, LLC, to the next level, and we are grateful. Hopefully, our

perseverance paved an easier path for others to create a microenterprise. We desire to help other parents of special needs young adults develop their gifts and be self-employed if they feel led.

It is a joy selling Caleb's paintings, ceramic dog dishes, greeting cards, and tote bags at the festivals. Andy and I are a good team as we are excited to share the journey. While the display of vibrant dog paintings catches people's attention, Caleb's miraculous story moves them. At the Winter Festival, we connected with a woman who cried as she shared that her son had the same diagnosis and died at 3.5 months old due to related complications. Emotional, she soaked in Caleb's hug, feeling as though her son was hugging her. It was an encounter that bonded us together like many others.

Recently, when I reached out to Caleb's physical therapist, Barb Hypes,

to ask permission to use her pictures, she congratulated me on writing the book. To my surprise, she said she received one of Caleb's greeting cards. She lives 170 miles away, but someone saw it in a store near Cedarburg and thought of her. What a beautiful full-circle moment! It made my heart smile to think of how far-reaching Caleb's testimony was through her therapy manual and his art!

Opportunities Abound

Dr. Treffert's wise counsel that we should pursue his art talent because it will lead to opportunities for Caleb is so true.

- At the Wine and Harvest Festival, we connected with the lead designer at Uniek / Kate and Laurel, a supplier of home decor products online and in-store. She was touched by his paintings and was interested in licensing some of his prints for wall art. Through Uniek, Caleb's prints are now available on Kate and Laurel, Amazon, and Overstock!

- An enlarged print of *Flowers in Bloom* is displayed at the Meriter Hospital lobby in Madison, Wisconsin.

- Caleb's *Flamingo Forward* was chosen to be on a tifo, a large banner in the soccer stadium, and a poster for the Forward Madison soccer match!

- *At Peace* was displayed at The Ridges Sanctuary in Baileys Harbor, Door County, Wisconsin.

Kate and Laurel collection

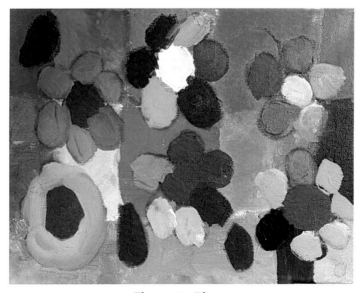

Flowers in Bloom

Flamingo Forward

Writing the Book

Ever since Caleb was very young, it was evident that God was at work. We saw miracle after miracle, and others were amazed as well. My mom and several friends strongly urged me to write a book. Utterly overwhelmed and collapsing from sheer exhaustion, I knew that I could not write it all down, and yet I knew I needed to capture the details before I forgot them. With the nudging from my dear friend, Rebecca, I bought a small handheld voice recorder and carried it in my purse for many years. As stories, mountain-top, and low-valley experiences happened, I recorded them. It was therapeutic even to share it aloud. Even though I didn't replay them, I just kept recording for years. As Caleb's business started to unfold and the busy mom season was easing up, I decided that I should at least start writing the book. I wanted to make sure that my mom and dad could read and enjoy the book since they prayed over Caleb the Conqueror.

My friend introduced me to her editor and publisher. Even though I wasn't ready to write the book, I wanted to see if this was "book-worthy." They wholeheartedly agreed that I should write the book. I said I didn't know if I had enough energy to set up Caleb's business and write a book simultaneously. Their advice clicked with me, "Those who are interested in Caleb's art will be interested in Caleb's story. And those who know Caleb's story will be interested in his art." Faced with the daunting challenge of writing a book, I eventually turned to

Come Unto Me

my voice recordings! Praise God that I had over 80 stories with fresh details and emotions. I could not have possibly remembered them. God graciously prompted me and others way back as the story unfolded.

Reflections

"My grace is sufficient for you, for My power is made perfect in weakness.
Therefore I will boast all the more gladly of my weaknesses,
so that the power may rest on me. That is why, for Christ's sake,
I delight in weaknesses, in insults, in hardships, in persecutions, in
difficulties. For when I am weak, then I am strong.

2 Corinthians 12:9-10

The day after Caleb was born, I was alone in the hospital room in the wee hours of the morning, crying out to God with a broken heart. The stillness of the morning was in stark contrast to the tsunami bombarding my thoughts. *This is not the plan we had for our baby.*

Reflections

When the doctor came in to check on me, I asked him what could have caused this. He put my mind at ease by saying we should not try to figure it out. His parting words were that it was a "medical mishap." Those words stuck with me. Andy and I don't believe it was a medical mishap. We believe that God entrusted us with Caleb.

As I reflect on my weeping morning and the gut-wrenching days and painful years that followed, I can attest that God's grace was, and still is, sufficient for me.

Every day is a new day, and His mercies are new every morning. He graciously carries us on this journey and sends us encouraging friends when we just *can't* anymore. As difficult as this journey is, the blessings and beautiful encounters far outweigh the hard times. We are awestruck at the miracles and see God at work in a real and powerful way.

His power is made perfect in our weakness. His power fortifies us and gives us the strength to carry on. It is His power that is made perfect in Caleb's weakness. It is His power that fortifies Caleb to be a Conqueror.

Chapter Resources:

Caleb Griswold Art Website: www.calebgriswold.com

Facebook: Paintings and Paws by Caleb
www.facebook.com/paintingsandpaws

Friendship Circle of Wisconsin
www.fcwi.org

Customized Self-Employment
www.dwd.wisconsin.gov/dvr/service-providers/tech-specs/cust-self-emp.htm

Jeanie Verschay - Employment Connections
www.jeanieverschay@gmail.com

Small Business Development Centers
www.sba.gov/local-assistance

Kate and Laurel
www.overstock.com/Caleb-Griswold,/k,/results.html?SearchType=Header

Strategies to Keep Your Sanity

Every child is unique and special. Our journey will not be yours; your challenges and struggles will differ. However, Andy and I pray that the strategies we have learned over the years will spark creativity and insight into how to avert meltdowns and prevent exasperating your child, other family members, and yourself. The strategies will be unique to your child's interests, capabilities, and resources available. The key is to study your child to discover what brings calmness, soothes his/her nervous system, and develops independence. Study yourself as well to know your limits, boundaries, and when you need to take a break. Both are equally important to know how to prevent burnout.

Lily Pads

Caleb's personality is sweet and kind, but if he gets "stuck" in a chaotic storm in his mind, he can fall apart quickly. Our mission is to preserve his dignity, especially if we are in public. We know Caleb would not melt down if he could help himself, so we handle him with care if we see the warning signs.

My creative ability to flex, pivot on demand, meet him where he is at, and maintain hope and joy comes from the Holy Spirit, so I continually need to draw my strength from Him. My hope is that these examples will foster new ideas to handle obsessions related to your circumstances and bring you peace and joy.

Strategies for Young Children

Recognize the warning signs

For Caleb, it was a high-pitched repetitive voice, red ears, and a quivering lip. We tried not to push him to the breaking point because we knew that, at that moment, he did not have the capability to gain his composure.

Negotiate

• "After you brush your teeth, we will take the dog for a walk."

Distract

• Take their hand, walk with them, and tell them a story.
• Point to something around you and ask them a question. "Is that dog playing with a stick?"

Redirect

• "Let's go outside and watch this dog play."
• "Did you see how many trucks passed by? Let's count them."

Sneak around

If Jesse needed to leave and didn't want Caleb to know, he had to sneak out the back door and go around the house. If he needed to bring food into the house and didn't want Caleb to see it, he had to sneak it in and hide it in his room which had a refrigerator.

Use nonverbal communication

Jesse innately understood how to play the "communication" game without words, just using a look, pointing, slight nod, wink, or writing a note. Jesse's motivation was he didn't want to wait for Caleb to calm down from a meltdown or see a situation escalate.

Use the word "no" sparingly

• Offer other options, all of which are acceptable.
  – "Would you like two crackers?" Break it in half.
  – "Yes, you can bring your toy." When they are distracted, hide it. Out of sight, out of mind.
• Distract and redirect.

Communicate with opposites

Jesse and I were usually on the same wavelength regarding Caleb. Jesse knew that when I said "yes" to Caleb, it often meant "no." What Caleb wanted at that moment was a fleeting thought, so saying "yes" appeased him. It was important for Jesse to understand this so that he wouldn't get upset over something that wouldn't happen anyway.

Walk ahead with the expectation they will follow

Bring closure for them
• Say "I'm sorry."
   Caleb needs to hear the words "I'm sorry." Even if it is insincere or a stretch to think of why we are apologizing, the words bring closure.
• "Finish coloring the sky, and then we will put it away."

Use humor
   Caleb didn't like to put his coat on, so my sister Brenda wore his coat to make him laugh.
• Talk with an accent.
• Pretend to trip.

Turn it into a game
• "Let's have a race to get dressed."

Praise often
• Be specific to reinforce good behavior.

Create a social story
   A social story is personalized for the child with the goal of understanding appropriate life skills. The story can be short.
• "We pull wagons, not hair."

Point out a good role model
   Caleb and Brenda would brush their teeth together over FaceTime.
• "Let's do what Brenda is doing."

Allow more time for them to process and transition
   Caleb put the brakes on when he felt rushed.

Provide deep sensory tools to soothe
   Caleb's sensory toolkit included items such as a weighted blanket, hammock, brushing therapy, therapy ball, headphones, and fidget toys.

Be flexible within the structure

Count inside of your head
• Force yourself to talk less while waiting. I counted.

Keep it positive

Give them a responsibility
   Caleb responded better when he could help in some way, even if it meant just holding the door.

Work alongside them to get started
• "I will write the first word, and you write the next one."

Use a checklist or a visual storyboard

Reward

Have someone other than you encourage them to finish the task

Pick your battles

Create a neutral phrase to communicate that they need a moment to regroup

"I'm having a watermelon moment."

This neutral phrase is a tool we created to help Caleb articulate when he/we recognized his mind was in a chaotic state. This phrase helped him to identify the chaos and take the emotion out of an emotionally charged situation. He would say, "I'm having a watermelon moment," when he felt he needed a break for whatever reason. Sometimes we asked him, "Are you having a watermelon moment?" when we thought he needed time and space. It was important not to push him or pressure him at that moment. Sometimes this worked; other times, it didn't, but it was another tool in his toolbox.

Create a "manual" with insights for teachers, babysitters, caregivers, and camp counselors. Understanding the nuances of your child can be a game changer

"Caleb's Manual"

When Caleb fixates on something, it is crucial to be proactive about changing the environment quickly so that the behavior doesn't get locked in his brain.

Caleb is consistently inconsistent.

When Caleb is obsessive and out of sorts, he is looking to bring order to his chaos and may come across as bossy.

Caleb is a hard worker and appears to be high functioning in many areas; however, he constantly works hard to make sense of his brain's input.

Caleb may appear manipulative, saying inappropriate responses, but he has significant expressive/receptive language issues. Assuming that he is being manipulative or deliberate creates a tense environment. It escalates a situation that may lead to chaos or confusion for him. It is not the time to push an agenda when approaching a chaotic state. It is time to de-escalate the situation with a calming attitude, approach, tone, words, body language, and possibly an alternate plan or expectation.

Strategies for Young Adults

Plan for a quick escape when someone else is home

• Leave slip-ons by the back door.

• Go for a power walk.

I love uninterrupted time in the morning so I can recharge. As soon as I hear the thump of Caleb's feet on the ground or the jingle of Xander's collar, I know to quietly slip on my shoes and sneak out the door. Caleb wants my attention from the moment he awakes, so I need to escape before he sees me.

• Go for a car ride.

I sneak out the door with my computer bag, cash, and keys.

Escape to Goodwill

One night as Caleb was having a meltdown, I escaped to Goodwill. I knew I looked pathetic in my pajamas and Andy's Birks, my go-to quick escape footwear choice. Of all people, I ran into our dear friends, Cathy and Mike, at Goodwill. They were a surprising distraction. We picked out a new outfit, complete with shoes, and I went out for the night with friends instead of going home.

Leave a book in the car to read while you wait for them to come out

Wherever you need them to move, make the next place more appealing than where they don't want to leave

In the mornings, Andy and I would say, "We are having a party in the garage," so that Caleb would want to come out of the house faster to get on the bus.

Find what motivates them

Caleb loves to go through a car wash. The extra cost for the tri-colored foam is worth every penny!

Teach them to shop independently

Sometimes while shopping, Caleb puts too many things in the cart. Since I don't want to make a scene, I usually buy it, hide it, and pull it out for a day when I need a break and want him to be entertained. After years of training to shop for healthy foods, he is pretty good at grocery shopping by himself. When he is done, I inspect his choices. Sometimes when I need to talk on the phone in privacy, I stay in the car while he grocery shops, and he calls me when he is ready for an inspection.

Purchase extra things as an incentive

Caleb hates to change his socks every day, so we buy him a lot of colorful dog socks to look forward to wearing every day of the week.

Use Amazon Alexa to your advantage

Caleb hates being in the bathroom alone, so Xander and Alexa are wonderful companions. He requests Alexa to sing songs and speak in other languages. He asks Alexa all his questions, and she doesn't get tired of answering him.

Don't make a big deal about certain behaviors; otherwise, they will become a big deal

• Resist the urge to ask rhetorical questions. "How many cupcakes did you eat??" What's done is done! Next time, hide the cupcakes. Sometimes you may regret asking rhetorical questions because it triggers them to obsess.

Creatively practice "out of sight, out of mind"

Caleb was picking at his skin, mainly his arms, so we bought nylon tattoos that covered his arms so he wouldn't think about it. He kept them on because he loved tattoos.

Hang on to things rather loosely

• Hide what you don't want to be used, destroyed, or eaten.

Think outside the box

Out of desperate need for a power nap one day, I suggested Caleb go to the laundromat to wash our comforter. He loved it and added it to his weekly schedule. Now, Caleb takes ownership of our laundry and even helps the janitor by cleaning out the lint traps. It is a win-win for everyone.

Encourage expressive outlets

Caleb's art room is an organized mess, but it is his own space that allows him to unwind and get lost in his creativity.

Organized Mess

Special Thanks

Andy, my supportive husband, whose gentle heart is devoted to loving his family. I cannot imagine being on this journey with anyone else. You let me be me and shine in my gifts, and I pray I do the same for you.

Jesse, our loving son, and the joy of our lives. We could not be more proud of the son, brother, and young man you are. God has a beautiful plan for your life, using your gifts and experiences. We are your biggest cheerleaders and prayer warriors.

My dear sisters – Brenda, my "mamma bear" sister, who steps into the nitty gritty details when life gets messy. Lynda, my "laugh until it hurts" sister, who makes me giggle when life is crazy. Your encouragement as sisters fills my soul.

Lori, my kindred spirit, who loves deeply with her loyal and God-fearing heart! Thank you for walking with me on this journey and helping me capture it in writing! Your hours of proofreading and caring friendship bless me beyond words.

Andy's family, for all of the love and support you have showered on us. We look forward to many more cherished family memories.

My mom and dad, for instilling a steadfast faith in God, teaching me to lean on Him fully and trust that His ways are higher than ours.

In Loving Memory...

Grandma and Grandpa Johnson
Great-Grandma and Great-Grandpa Lepak
We are forever grateful for their
dedication and generous hearts.

Visiting Cardinals

About the Author

A teacher at heart and by training, Laura enjoys building relationships, incorporating creativity, and being a trailblazer in many areas of her life. She is a strong advocate for her special needs son, Caleb, and his self-employment at Paintings and Paws by Caleb, LLC. Her faith is her foundation, and the joy of the Lord is her strength. Laura loves creating memories with her loving husband, Andy, and two beautiful sons. She is passionate about sharing their family's journey, strategies, and resources to bring hope to others.

Follow Laura:

Facebook - Paintings and Paws by Caleb
https://www.facebook.com/paintingsandpaws

Caleb Griswold Art Website: calebgriswold.com

email: paintingsandpaws@gmail.com